The Second Media Age

Mark Poster

Polity Press

Copyright © Mark Poster 1995

The right of Mark Poster to be identified as
author of this work has been asserted in accordance with the
Copyright, Designs and Patents Act 1988.

First published in 1995 by Polity Press
in association with Blackwell Publishers Ltd.

Reprinted 1996

Editorial office:
Polity Press
65 Bridge Street
Cambridge CB2 1UR, UK

Marketing and production:
Blackwell Publishers Ltd
108 Cowley Road
Oxford OX4 1JF, UK

Published in the USA by
Blackwell Publishers Inc.
238 Main Street
Cambridge MA 02142, USA

ISBN 0–7456–1395–0
ISBN 0–7456–1396–9 (pbk)

A CIP catalogue record for this book is available from the British Library and the
Library of Congress.

Typeset in 10½ on 12 pt Sabon
by Best-set Typesetter Ltd., Hong Kong
Printed in Great Britain by Hartnolls Ltd, Bodmin, Cornwall

This book is printed on acid-free paper

Contents

For Carol

Acknowledgements

Many people deserve my thanks for comments and suggestions with this book. Members of the Critical Theory Institute continue to serve me as a unique academic environment in which critique is forthright but constructive. Over the years relations of trust have grown there which nurture intellectual development and discussion. My friend and colleague Jon Wiener gave me excellent advice on several of the chapters. Rob Kling read several chapters, offering valuable suggestions, and made me aware of many new works on topics I treat. Versions of the chapters were presented at many campuses and conventions at which I received much valuable criticism which I accepted as gracefully as I was able and for which I am very grateful. Ideas for this volume were also formed in my classes. Graduate students in History and in UC Irvine's Emphasis in Critical Theory were often more helpful than they can know in assisting me to clarify issues, discover new texts and revise old assumptions. Carol Starcevic provided assiduous, helpful readings of many chapters.

Earlier versions of certain chapters appeared first as follows: chapters 1 and 2 in *Arena journal* (September 1994); chapter 3 in David Crowley and David Mitchell, eds, *Communication Theory Today* (New York: Blackwell, 1993), pp. 173–92; chapter 4 in Wolfgang Natter, ed., *Contemporary Democratic Theory and Democracy* (New York: Guilford, forthcoming, 1995); chapter 5 in *Modern Fiction Studies* 38: 3 (1992), pp. 567–80; chapter 6 in Douglas Kellner, ed., *Baudrillard: A Critical Reader* (New York: Blackwell, 1994); chapter 7 in *Paradigm*; chapter 8 in *Zone: Incorporations* 6 (Spring 1992), pp. 436–40; chapter 9 in *New German Critique* 53 (Spring–Summer 1991), pp. 131–48; chapter 10 in *Cultural Critique* 19 (Fall 1991), pp. 217–22.

PART I

THEORETICAL RECONSIDERATIONS

1

Social Theory and the New Media

The twentieth century has witnessed the introduction of communications systems that allow a wide distribution of messages from one point to another, conquering space and time first through electrification of analogue information, then through digitalization. Among critical social theorists there has been a debate over the political effects of these technologies, with one side (Benjamin, Enzensberger, McLuhan) arguing for potential democratization and the other side (Adorno, Habermas, Jameson) seeing the dangers to liberty as predominant.[1] This debate occurred at a time when the broadcast model of communications prevailed. In film, radio and television, a small number of producers sent information to a large number of consumers. With the incipient introduction of the information "superhighway" and the integration of satellite technology with television, computers and telephone, an alternative to the broadcast model, with its severe technical constraints, will very likely enable a system of multiple producers/distributors/consumers, an entirely new configuration of communication relations in which the boundaries between those terms collapse. A second age of mass media is on the horizon. At this critical junction, I shall review the debate over the relation between technology, culture and politics of the first media age, gauging the extent of the value of those positions for an analysis of an emerging new technocultural arrangement. Although one portion of this discussion, the Adorno–Benjamin debate on mass culture, has been analyzed many times, I shall focus on the issue of communications technology, a topic which has been largely overlooked. I shall concentrate my attention on the problem of the construction of the subject in relation to these technologies, the issue of the body and the question of postmodernity. Throughout the chapter my chief concern shall be the development of a critical social theory that accounts for the impending massive cultural reorganizations of the second media age. My motivation is neither to celebrate nor to condemn these prospects but to indicate their importance for cultural change.

The general political question that haunts the discussion of the media for critical social theory is the stalled dialectic. The parties to the debate acknowledge the absence of an oppositional political force that might challenge the status quo. For some the working class, in whom much hope was placed by Marxist theory, has been politically nullified to no small extent by the media but in the widest sense was assimilated into modern society as part of a baleful mass. For others modern society achieved an integration of the working class largely without overt political repression, through the operations of what Antonio Gramsci termed "hegemony."[2] While these positions have a great deal in common, their difference lies in how the popular groups are regarded: in the former the working class has become an inert mass, manipulated by the media and popular culture generally. For the latter the dominant forces have been able to establish a statis but resistance continues at the micro-level of everyday life. The first position is characteristic of most members of the Frankfurt School; the latter is typical of the cultural studies group and of Michel de Certeau in France. Feminists and postcolonial theorists align themselves on either side of the issue. The question I wish to raise is to what extent does the debate hinge on a certain understanding of technology, one characteristic of the broadcast phase of its development which is in the process of being supplanted by a much different configuration?

I   Critical Social Theory Confronts the First Media Age

Representative of the general attitude of the majority of intellectuals toward the electronic media, writer and critic Georges Duhamel refers to the cinema as "a pastime for helots, a diversion for the uneducated, wretched, worn-out creatures who are consumed by their worries . . . , a spectacle which requires no concentration and presupposes no intelligence . . . , which kindles no light in the heart and awakens no hope other than the ridiculous one of someday becoming a 'star' in Los Angeles."[3] With these harsh words Duhamel expresses his revulsion toward mass culture, finding in it no redeeming value, not even in some small corner. His judgment blankets the entire extent of the domain, disbursing an even intolerance without the slightest qualification. His stance emits a steadfast disgust, remarkable in its purity and consistency. Surely not all intellectuals who found fault with movies and other electronic communications systems were as absolute in their condemnation. But many have been just as negative, just as scornful, even those who have had politically motivated sympathy for the consumers of these media and interests in the quality of daily life; those, in other words, who located the hopes of mankind for emancipation from domination in the vicissitudes of common folk. For modernist intellectuals, cultural capital or distinction in Bourdieu's sense[4] varies inversely with one's contact with the media.

Duhamel's characterization of film bespeaks the viewpoint of the intellectual and artistic elite of modernity, consigning the masses to the unrelieved hell of popular culture. His bleak portrait enacts a division between his own tastes and those of everyman and everywoman; it installs a boundary around the art that he enjoys and relegates everything else (film, radio and television) to a valueless nether world that is little different from commerce, industry and other regions of modernity. Duhamel incorporates the media into the general contempt which many artists and intellectuals display toward modern society in general. One function of this contempt is to preserve high culture as separate and precious. For the Duhamels of the twentieth century, I contend, this contempt is more significantly motivated by the deep need to reject the media *a priori*, without careful investigation, because something about it threatens their identity as intellectuals. This attitude, I suggest, continues today among many, especially in the disciplines of the humanities, foreclosing a sustained inquiry into the media that is attentive to the enormous fascination they hold for so many people. I suggest further that something about what I call the first media epoch, the one dominated by the broadcast model of few producers and many consumers of messages, offends the intellectual's sense of authorship and that this is so regardless of the qualities that pertain to the cultural objects in question. *First epoch media unsettle the autonomous subject of modernity*. Intellectuals of this period were and are largely incapable of receiving messages in the form of film, radio and television. And this failure prevented the critical social theorists among this group from estimating the changes in the culture of the majority of the population, particularly in its relation to politics.

Even a cursory glance at the writings of the Frankfurt School confirms this judgment. Writers in the *Zeitschrift für Sozialforschung* probed the workings of the capitalist economy and liberal ideology with subtlety and sophistication. Whatever disgust they may have harbored for modern industrial organizations and institutions of the nation-state did not prevent them from looking closely and effectively at their workings, from extracting a nuanced account of what were, in their terms, the benefits and the costs of these activities, and their consequences for the project of enlightenment. Such was not the case when it came to examining the media. Here judgments lost their acuity and descended into polemic and vituperation. In perhaps the best and most influential example of Frankfurt School writing on the media, Adorno and Horkheimer, in *Dialectic of Enlightenment,* betray the insensitivity of the modernist intellectual for the cultural experiences of the population. They first note the chief technological character of the first media age: "The technical contrast between the few production centers and the large number of widely dispersed consumption . . ." (p. 121). Next they indicate their difficulty with the situation of the subject in the modern media: "The step from the telephone to the radio has clearly distinguished the roles. The former still allowed the subscriber to play the role of subject, and was liberal. The latter is democratic: it turns all participants into listeners and authoritatively subjects them to broadcast programs which are all exactly the same . . . (p. 122). The gigantic fact that speech penetrates everywhere replaces its content . . . The inherent tendency of radio is to make the speaker's word, the false commandment, absolute. A recommendation becomes an order" (p. 159).[5] For Adorno and Horkheimer the broadcast model of the first media age was the practical equivalent to fascism.[6]

Ten years later Adorno wrote an essay on television with very much the same results. Reactions to television are not those of the "liberal" subject, independent and reflective, but are unconscious and massified: "The repetitiveness, the selfsameness, and the ubiquity of modern mass culture tend to make for automatized reactions and to weaken the forces of individual resistance."[7] Adorno attributes to the purely technological features of the broadcast system – the ability to disseminate widely and instantaneously an identical information signal – the effect of reversing the project of Enlightenment. On a slightly more positive side the media, to Adorno, are a force of solidarity in an increasingly diffuse society: "The more inarticulate and diffuse the audience of modern mass media seems to be, the more mass media tend to achieve their 'integration'" (p. 220). But the "integration" is placed in quotes, suggesting its inauthenticity, and Adorno continues the argument with a strong whiff of Duhamel's revulsion: ". . . the majority of television shows today aim at producing . . . the very smugness, intellectual passivity, and gullibility that seem to fit in with totalitarian creeds, even if the explicit surface message of the shows may be antitotalitarian" (p. 222). In an unacknowledged behaviorist flurry and without any empirical basis but his own imperial authority, Adorno concludes his jeremiad with a statement that the consequence of the media on the population is a dumb stupefaction: "The more stereotypes become reified and rigid in the present setup of cultural industry, the less people are likely to change their preconceived ideas with the progress of their experience" (p. 229).

Perhaps the epitome of Adorno's position on the media came in "On the Fetish-Character in Music and the Regression of Listening," an essay from 1938,[8] well before he developed the concept of the culture industry. If Adorno had any area of expertise outside of philosophy, it was music, and his conclusions about contemporary music are stark. At stake is nothing less than "the liquidation of the individual" (p. 276). In this essay Adorno extends Marx's analysis of the fetishism of commodities to the domain of music appreciation, as in the following example: "The consumer is really worshipping the money that he himself has paid for the ticket to the Toscanini concert" (p. 278). If the "fetish-character in music" is explained by classic Marxist concepts extended to the cultural domain, the "regression in listening" requires the innovation of technological determinism. Adorno's discussion of listening shifts genres from classical to popular music and relies primarily on the radio as causal agent: "Regressive listening is tied to production by the machinery of distribution . . ." (p. 287). The media of the radio producers "deconcentrated" listeners who use/abuse music as background noise or "mere" entertainment. The apotheosis of "fetishism" and "regression" occurs again through the influence of technology: "Of all fetishistic listeners, the radio ham is perhaps the most complete. It is irrelevant to him what he hears or even how he hears; he is only interested in the fact that he hears. . . . With the same attitude, countless radio listeners play with the feedback or the sound dial . . ." (p. 293). For Adorno, then, radio destroys musical taste, lowers the level of general culture and contributes to the possible demise of democracy.

In response John Mowitt contends that in Adorno's critique of distracted listening the subject presupposed by him is the vision-dominated subject of the print era. Relying very much on McLuhan's theory of the sensory transformation of the media, Mowitt argues that electronic media "reintegrate" the senses, effectively nullifying the basis of Adorno's position.[9] For my purposes the value of Mowitt's essay is that it underscores the unreflected and limited figure of the subject in Adorno's theory of the media, one that greatly detracts from its ability to develop a critical theory of that domain.

The very serious question for critical social theory at stake in Adorno and Horkheimer's remarks on radio and television is the relation between technology and culture. Without raising this issue at the general level, they argue that technology, in this case radio, in itself determines its effect. Because it is a one-way transmission with no reply possible, radio produces a language of command. Surprisingly these advocates of total human liberation emerge as technological determinists. In their effort to understand how the culture of capitalism undermines the dialectic, how it transforms the working class from a potentially revolutionary subject into a passive consumer, a decidedly conservative political force, Adorno and Horkheimer bypass the cultural level in favor of technological determinism. In their analysis they configure the working class or the popular forces as passive and inert, mirroring the critique that they desire to provide. Their logic runs: (1) since World War I, the working class has not been a politically effective negation of capitalism; (2) the "culture industry" mediates between the relations of production and politics, defusing the dialectic; (3) a chief reason for its success are the electronic media which introduce authoritarian voices in everyday life. The radio monologue is their *deus ex machina*, a magical device that transforms free agents into passive victims. Behind this logic, I contend, lies the problematic binary of the subject as autonomous/heteronomous: if the subject as radio audience cannot enter the dialogue, according to Adorno and Horkheimer, it is unfree. If the process of subject constitution in media communications were comprehended without this binary, a more complex, nuanced and perhaps less bleak conclusion might emerge from the analysis, one that might account for the cultural level of reception and modulate the rigid determinism of radio technology. Bound to the logocentric subject of modern theory, Adorno and Horkheimer are unable to see the popular audience of radio as anything other than heteronomous and therefore attribute this enslavement to the technology.[10]

Technology itself, even the technology of cultural reproduction, did not necessarily evoke such animus from Adorno. His discussion of the phonograph, for example, is balanced and not blind to certain benefits of the device. In reference to the phonograph Adorno writes, "The ambiguity of the results of forward-moving technology . . . confirms the ambiguity of the process of forward-moving rationality as such."[11] Adorno admitted certain benefits of technological mediation, almost exclusively, it must be noted, in the domain of classical music. And these benefits, it must also be noted, hinge upon the ability of the phonograph to confirm and even enhance the consumer's character as an autonomous, critical subject. The phonograph permits the permanent recording of music, saving it from oblivion and permitting the listener repeated auditions.[12] Adorno comprehended the technological basis of the phonograph record (inscriptions in vinyl analogous to sound waves). He also discovered that the long-playing record permitted the uninterrupted listening to a complete movement of Beethoven's Third Symphony, concluding that on this basis alone it deserved praise.[13] But his recognition of the virtues of long-playing records came in 1969, almost two decades after their inception. In a well-researched essay regarding Adorno's position on the media, Thomas Levin calls attention to these anomalies, as well as others concerning film and radio, regarding them as a basis to "reconsider his position on mass media and technology in general."[14] While it is good to learn that Adorno's hostility to the mass media was not hardfast, the critical theorist might do better, I contend, in analyzing his deep limitations on the question of technology because they are more characteristic and have had infinitely wider impact. The purpose of doing so, however, is not to condemn the person or even belittle his extraordinary theoretical abilities but to develop further the interpretive powers of critical theory.

The type of intellectual which Adorno represents shies away from media culture and from technology in general in order to preserve the position of the autonomous subject. Adorno was quite aware of this defensive posture. In the introduction to *Minima Moralia* he wrote with remarkable reflexivity, "For since the overwhelming objectivity of historical movement in its present phase consists so far only in the dissolution of the subject, without yet giving rise to a new one, individual experience necessarily bases itself on the old subject, now historically condemned, which is still for-itself, but no longer in-itself."[15] Trapped within the binary autonomy/heteronomy, Adorno saw no alternative to the modernist subject: either that subject existed or it was "dissolved" leaving no subject at all, just a mere thing, an inert mass. This degree zero of the subject, one who is only "for-itself" hovering above social space in a remote cloud of critique, was an outcome, Adorno thought, of the twin scourges of the twentieth century – both the culture industry and fascism: "In face of the totalitarian unison with which the eradication of difference is pro-claimed as a purpose in itself, even part of the social force of libera-tion may have temporarily withdrawn to the individual sphere. If critical theory lingers there, it is not only with a bad conscience."[16]

In these passages, Adorno at once recognizes the subject as histori-cally constructed and pulls back from that recognition. The "objectiv-ity of the historical moment" liquidates the subject and no "new one" has appeared. These phrases suggest that subjects are constructed and destroyed in social conditions, although no specific mechanisms of the process are here indicated. In other places, as we have seen above, technologies such as the radio and film are endowed with the powers of subject dissolution. Adorno recognizes the phenomena of war as an accelerator of such practices. In the following example, he goes so far as to name "experience" itself as a casualty of new communica-tions technologies under conditions of war:

> The total obliteration of the war by information, propaganda, com-mentaries, with camera-men in the first tanks and war reporters dying heroic deaths, the mish-mash of enlightened manipulation of public opinion and oblivious activity: all this is another expression for the withering of experience, the vacuum between men and their fate, in which their real fate lies. It is as if the reified, hardened plaster-cast of events takes the place of events themselves. Men are reduced to walk-on parts in a monster documentary film which has no spectators, since the least of them has his bit to do on the screen.[17]

In this perspective, war and communications technologies are a frightful duo. One recalls the film *The Great Man* (1957), in which America's favorite media personality, now reporting on the war from the front lines, is revealed as a fraud who used advanced technology to dub in sounds from the battlefield while he remained in safety in the rear. Like Adorno, the film depicts war and communications technologies as "dehumanizing," instead of understanding the pro-cess, as Paul Virilio does in *War and Cinema*, as a process of reconfiguration, not one of pure loss: "*For men at war, the function of the weapon is the function of the eye.* It is therefore quite understandable that, after 1914, the air arm's violent cinematic disruption of the space continuum, together with the lightning advances of military technology, should have literally exploded the old homogeneity of vision and replaced it with the heterogeneity of perceptual fields."[18]

I submit that Adorno's inability to theorize the new condition of social space filled with combinations of machines and humans, together with his adherence to the binary of the subject as autonomous/heteronomous, pre-empted his analysis of the subject as being reconstituted by media culture as well as the activity of the process of reception. I offer two steps toward the clearing out of this problem. First, the linguistic turn in its poststructuralist form enables the theorist to posit the subject as constituted in social space without privileging the modernist form of the subject. The subject may then be decentered or multiple or whatever without being "dissolved." Second, as in *The Mode of Information*,[19] this interpretive stance is applied to the electronic technologies of communication to explore the specific patterns of subject constitution in the recent period. No prejudice against machines, the quality of material presented on the media or the general level of culture of participating individuals encumbers this analysis. The goal is not to evaluate the quality of the subjects constituted by the media but to open an analysis of their forms and to do so in such a way that the inherent mechanisms of domination may be revealed. These mechanisms are to be understood not as limiting the autonomy of a pre-existing subject but as interfering with the process through which subjects recognize that they are constituted and that they may, with the proper mediations of others, reconstitute themselves and their world so that subject constitution becomes its designated goal and social end.

II Adorno Is Not Alone

So powerful are Duhamel's disgust and Adorno and Horkheimer's technological determinism of the media that they are also found, it is worth noting in passing, in some theorists who have made a serious effort to overcome the logocentric subject and the binary of autonomy/heteronomy, taking a linguistic turn toward a different understanding of the constitution of the subject. Such is the case of

Louis Althusser in his important essay "Ideology and Ideological State Apparatuses," where he denigrates the determining force of the media as follows: "The communications apparatus by cramming every 'citizen' with daily doses of nationalism, chauvinism, liberalism, moralism, etc., by means of the press, the radio and television."[20] In Althusser's version the media are not so much technological determinisms as emanations of a determining bourgeois ideology, itself reflecting the bourgeois class position in the capitalist mode of production.

In his early work *The Structural Transformation of the Public Sphere*, Jürgen Habermas simply repeated the conclusions of Adorno and Horkheimer. In the constitution of public opinion, he wrote, "one finds the often discussed things generated as self-evident by the culture industry, the ephemeral results of the relentless publicist barrage and propagandist manipulation by the media to which consumers are exposed . . ."[21] The gradual emergence of a public sphere since the eighteenth century was eventually threatened by electronic media, Habermas here argues, which nullify its democratizing potentials.

Like Adorno and Horkheimer, Habermas attempts to theorize the domain of culture with a view to understanding its relation to politics and to its effects upon the project of emancipation. In distinction from the older generation of the Frankfurt School, however, Habermas, in his more recent work, developed a theory of culture or symbolic interaction which locates the point of critique in the "lifeworld," the egalitarian space of the everyday rather than in the elite moment of high culture or in the philosophical labor of "negative dialectics." For Habermas "mutual understanding" requires "the universal validity claims" which are inherent in all speech situations, these serving as an ontological bulwark for the creation of a democratic public sphere. The media extend rather than restrict this potential: "Writing, the printing press and electronic media mark the significant innovations . . . by these means speech acts are freed from spatiotemporal contextual limitations and made available for multiple and future contexts." Communicative action, he continues, is "raised again to a higher power by the electronic media of mass communication developed in the twentieth century."[22]

In an important sense, then, this theory of communicative action prevents Habermas from dismissing the media as easily as his intellectual forebears. While noting the same problem as they did, that of unidirectional speech in the media, Habermas discerns a different possibility.

... media publics hierarchize and at the same time remove restrictions on the horizon of possible communication. The one aspect cannot be separated from the other – and therein lies their ambivalent potential. Insofar as mass media one-sidedly channel communication flows in a centralized network – from the center to the periphery or from above to below – they considerably strengthen the efficacy of social controls. But tapping this authoritarian potential is always precarious because there is a counterweight of emancipatory potential built into communication structures themselves. Mass media can simultaneously contextualize and concentrate processes of reaching understanding but it is only in the first instance that they relieve interaction from yes/no responses to criticizable validity claims. Abstracted and clustered though they are, these communications cannot be reliably shielded from the possibility of opposition by responsible actors.[23]

For Habermas, what saves the media from complete authoritarian, technological determinism is not that they mark an alternative to the logocentric subject but rather that they institute an even stronger version of it, one enhanced by the recognition that the technology itself contains liberatory elements. Habermas acknowledges the "emancipatory potential" of the media in the sense that they bring information to a large audience. But even so this admission is grudging on his part since he generally condemns the media for not permitting validity claims to emerge, only "yes/no responses." The media for him are certainly not "an ideal speech situation" or a democratic public sphere. However, since human beings are so powerfully constituted as "responsible actors," even if only in Habermas's theory, they are, he thinks, capable of resisting the media.

III Benjamin's Concept of Technoculture

Walter Benjamin's "The Work of Art in the Age of Mechanical Reproduction" (1936)[24] departs dramatically from the perspectives we have been exploring. First, Benjamin, educated in the same traditions of high modernist art as Duhamel, Adorno and the rest, nonetheless manages to avoid disdain for the cultural products disseminated by electronic media. Second, although he is animated by a Marxist version of the project of Enlightenment and he is interested in the way culture has intervened in the historical dialectic, Benjamin does not transpose a disgust for the common into an explanation of clogged historical conditions. Third, he does not bring a logocentric view of the subject into his understanding of the media. Like Adorno, Benjamin is deeply mindful of the ability of popular forces to resist hegemonic structures.[25] Yet he avoids introducing the binary of autonomy/heteronomy into his analysis of the effects of the media on the formation of the proletariat. Fourth, he wrestles in large part successfully with the question of the relation of technology and culture, avoiding the trap of technological determinism. The major advance, one might say, in Benjamin's essay is the omission of the problematic aspects one routinely finds in the discussion of the media by social theorists of his time and well beyond it. As a result he is able to address the question of film in a manner that begins to consider its specific technical and cultural qualities, as well as their relation to politics.[26] I now turn to a review of Benjamin's argument in order to assess its ability to offer a critical theory of the mass media in its first age.

Benjamin is aware of the egalitarian impetus of the media. Film, for him, brings works of art to the people. By its physical setting, art before the media remained remote from everyday life and, by its internal design, aloof from the lower classes. This "aura" surrounding works of art evaporates when art is reproduced many times and dispersed throughout social space, even appearing in working-class districts. Once the work of art is placed closer to the people, its mediation by the technology, in a parallel but opposite way, serves to distance the audience from the performance, shifting the point of identification from the performer to the technology. In film the audience takes the position of the camera, not of the actors, promoting, Benjamin contends, a critical stance. Furthermore, he argues that the principle of the media is that the author and the audience are in reversible, not fixed and hierarchical, positions, undermining one of the chief means by which art championed, even against its will, authoritarian politics. In addition, the collective and simultaneous conditions of viewing film, he maintains, encourage both critical and receptive attitudes. Finally, film for him promotes analytic habits because "what is represented can be easily isolated," and therefore may be read closely.

These features of the media promote equality and liberty for Benjamin. But they are not simply aspects of the technology; rather they are aspects of the way the technology is actualized in the culture.[27] Films could be limited to a single copy and shown only in restricted locations, for example. In this case they would not be brought closer to the masses and they might retain their aura, as in fact many "art" films do even today. Benjamin is very aware that the media are themselves also mediated by the major social institutions, especially capitalism. He contrasts, perhaps wrongly, the Soviet films of Eisenstein with those of Hollywood, indicating how the latter promote the star system with its "illusionist spectacles." In fact, for Benjamin, the potential democratizing advances of the media are all reversible according to the manner of their realization. There is no automatic guarantee for him of any particular political direction of the media. Technological determinism is thereby excluded from his analysis. Benjamin is able to formulate his view of the media in an intermediate zone between technology and culture, although he does not explicitly theorize this dimension of his work. Unencumbered by the elitist and humanist assumptions of Duhamel and Adorno, Benjamin interprets the media of the first age far more expertly than they do: the potentials for freedom are examined in the context of the play of forces in the current conjuncture. He neither dismisses the media as bourgeois detritus nor celebrates their arrival as the onset of utopia.

In the heyday of the New Left, some 34 years after the appearance of Benjamin's essay, Hans Magnus Enzensberger published "Constituents of a Theory of Media," echoing many of Benjamin's themes but also flattening out the ambivalence and complexity of the earlier account. Within the context of determinist treatments of the media, Enzensberger portrays the exact opposite image to that of Adorno: the media determine a progressive political impulse and constitute egalitarian, free subjects. In addition Enzensberger lacks Adorno's repugnance toward things popular. His essay, important in its day as one of the few theoretical works by a socialist in the West on the media, illustrates the problems of over-enthusiasm toward the undeniably novel features of media society. Here are some examples which illustrate the problem: "The open secret of the electronic media . . . is their mobilizing power . . . the media are making possible mass participation in a social and socialized productive process . . . the media are . . . an immense threatening power . . . *for the first time* [emphasis added] they present a basic challenge to bourgeois culture . . ."[28] The degree to which the media actively mediate communication relations is here easily forgotten faced with the breathless possibilities they open up. Although Enzensberger recognizes the problem of what he calls "manipulation" by the media, he quickly dismisses the difficulty in favor of a representationalist attitude in which the media are merely tools, transparently reflecting the messages they transmit. He fails to see the media as new language formations, structuring subjects in determined ways beneath the intentions of senders and receivers of information. He also does not confront the issue, as Benjamin did, of the technical constraints of the broadcast model of the media.

IV   Baudrillard on the Culture of the Media

Jean Baudrillard presents an interesting problem for the analysis I am undertaking. He is as cognizant as Benjamin of the cultural implications of the media and just as fascinated with the possibilities they suggest for a future society. But he is at times as revolted by popular culture as Adorno. He refers to contemporary culture as a form of "obscenity," very much in the spirit of Adorno or Marcuse, an obscenity "where the most intimate processes of our life become the virtual feeding ground of the media . . ."[29] The PBS series on the Loud family of Santa Barbara serves as his example – examples which are often, too often, taken from the culture of the United States.[30] To compare Adorno's and Baudrillard's remarks on aspects of culture in the United States would be a study in the virtuosity of European snobbery. Yet Baudrillard, unlike Adorno, relentlessly stares at the screen, determined to discover the basis of its fascination.

For Baudrillard the media undermine modern society and the modern subject; they refute the logic of representation, the binary of freedom/determinism, above all, the figure of the free subject. He writes, "Now the media are nothing else than a marvelous instrument for destabilizing the real and the true, all historical or political truth . . . the addiction we have for the media, the impossibility of doing without them . . . is not a result of a desire for culture, communication, and information, but of this perversion of truth and falsehood, of this destruction of meaning in the operation of the medium. The desire for a show, the desire for simulation . . . is a spontaneous, total resistance to the ultimatum of historical and political reason."[31] For Baudrillard, the media install a new culture in the heart of everyday life, one outside the Enlightenment opposition of reason and the irrational. Television, for example, does not oppose itself to reason. Quite to the contrary, television provides information, doing so instantaneously and ubiquitously, inaugurating an age when, by merely depressing the power button on the remote control, anyone can have knowledge of world affairs.

If Baudrillard was at times troubled by the monologic nature of the broadcast media,[32] for the most part he rejected that strategy as one which remains within the logic of the modern, searching for true subjects of speech. If film, radio and television were "speech without response," as he once complained in "Requiem for the Media" and as Adorno could never forget, generally Baudrillard was rather more interested in the way the media played with what is termed "reality" by liberals and Marxists and what he calls "the social." For him the media are strange phenomena, ones that simply cannot fit within modern distinction of the real and the imaginary. The media produce only simulations and remain in that register: they create both intensifications of reality and substitutes for reality without ever attaining it. When popular enough as they are today, they incite a thirst for reality. Hence all the television shows which bring reality into a fictional setting, shows about "real" murders, "real" bloopers, "infomercials," and so forth.

Baudrillard's favorite though perhaps unexpected example of the media are opinion polls (pp. 208ff). Like film, radio and television, opinion polls institute a level of simulation into daily life. For Baudrillard the opinion poll "is a compound, a mixture of two heterogeneous systems whose data cannot be transferred from one to the other. An operational system which is statistical, information-based, and simulational is projected onto a traditional values system, onto a system of representation, will and opinion" (p. 209). Opinion polls construct knowledge on the basis of rules of statistics and questionnaire strategies. This knowledge would not otherwise exist in the social. The mode of existence of political opinion before the electronic media was very different from that of opinion polls. Opinion was formed through reading newspapers and through speech. In the Ancien Régime, the French king would learn the opinion of a town about his rule by sending to the place an emissary on horse, who simply gauged the response of the people to his presence. Although face-to-face speech and printed newspapers are still "mediations," they do not construct simulations which disrupt and refute the modern social logic of representation. Hence for Baudrillard the crucial feature of the media is that they introduce a cultural principle which does not fit into any form of the modern.

In addition to introducing a new cultural principle, the media, for Baudrillard, play havoc with modern practices and conceptions of politics. Both liberals and Marxists think that individuals have real needs, whether based on natural rights theory or the notion of species-being. For both positions individuals are whole, centered subjects *upon whom* structures of domination are imposed. Emancipation consists of removing unwanted and unnecessary impositions. Now the media are often understood by liberals and Marxists in just such terms, as additions which oppress or manipulate individuals with "irrational" advertisements, violence and sexuality. Baudrillard, on the contrary, contends "that there is no relationship between a system of meaning and a system of simulation . . . they do not act in the time-space of will and of representation in which judgment is formed" (p. 209). To the degree that the analyst does not account for the special logic of simulation, the relationship of the media to politics remains obscure. Continuing his line of argumentation, Baudrillard thinks the media construct a politics of the object, as opposed to that of the subject, in which the masses take on the logic of the object as a form of resistance, in the way children resist being submissive objects of their parents' will by a strategy of hyper-submission, super-conformity. Here I think Baudrillard too quickly fills a gap in his position. One can say that the media introduce a new political register without specifying how that register will develop a logic of resistance. I suspect Baudrillard's theory of resistance by "the silent majority" as object is a simple reversal of modernity's insistence on the subject. In this respect Baudrillard remains within the binary object/subject as a theoretical articulation, failing to account for the manner in which the media, as postmodern practices, will stimulate a new politics.

V The Second Media Age – Two-Way, Decentralized Communication

Baudrillard's writings allow us to interrogate the broadcast media at the level of their cultural articulation; we are not limited to asking, as Adorno does, how one-way speech is fascist, especially when it is controlled by capitalists. With Baudrillard we can see that no one "controls" the cultural logic of the media, which he sees rather as antagonizing and disrupting modern practices and discourses. By outlining a logic of simulation, Baudrillard's writings form a transition to a second media age, one in which the constraints of broadcasting will be breached so that the politics of the media can emerge in other than modernist terms. Thereby the new media may be seen as creating a major force that is uncontainable by modern positions.

Baudrillard's work remains infused with a sense of the media as unidirectional, and therefore does not anticipate the imminent appearance of bidirectional, decentralized media, such as the Internet, with its new opportunities for reconstructing the mechanisms of subject constitution. Nonetheless Baudrillard does overcome the chief limitation in most other approaches to the popular media: the imposition upon them of the modernist notion of the autonomy of art. For many of his critics, Baudrillard's great crime is his failure to impose Kantian or modernist standards of aesthetic evaluation upon media culture.[33] The best statement of chagrin at the new circumstances is again given by Adorno: ". . . a change in the character of the art commodity itself is coming about. What is new is not that it is a commodity, but that today it deliberately admits it is one; that art renounces its own autonomy and proudly takes its place among consumption goods . . ."[34] The admission by art of its commodity status entails the abdication of "purposelessness." Adorno continues, "The purposelessness of the great modern work of art depends on the anonymity of the market." And the advantage of purposelessness, one must presume, is that it overcomes the chief limitation of bourgeois culture, its purposefulness, its small-minded utilitarianism, its efficiency obsessed instrumentality, its dehumanizing performativity. With the postmodern collapse of the high art/mass culture divide, Baudrillard's acceptance of the new conditions places him, for diehard modernists, in the camp of the enemy.

Baudrillard also to some extent overcomes another major difficulty with the earlier discussion: its configuration of the relation of human and machine. Since *Fatal Strategies* (1983) he has proposed abandoning logics of the subject in favor of those of "the object." His somewhat ambiguous argument, betraying traces of what I would like to call "reverse humanism," moving from the position of the subject to that of the object, is considerably surpassed by those who are rethinking the relation of humans to machines, such as Gilles Deleuze, Félix Guattari, Donna Haraway and others. Guattari writes: ". . . today's information and communication machines do not merely convey representational contents, but also contribute to the fabrication of new *assemblages* of enunciation, individual and collective."[35] This implies a refunctioning of the categories of individual, social and machine in a manner that allows their mutual imbrication to be investigated. The problem for critical theory then is to develop theoretical strategies that erase the humanist subject and bypass the human/non-human opposition. Canguilhem suggests that "the construction of machines can indeed be understood by virtue of certain truly biological principles,"[36] thereby crossing the line of the living and the dead. Hillel Schwartz imagines a theory of kinesis that cuts through the divide of machine and organism, opposing a "modernist" understanding of contemporary movement as machinic: "dissociated, fetishized, ultimately empty."[37] And Manuel DeLanda brazenly announces the uselessness of older categorical distinctions by affirming an analytic of "nonorganic life."[38] But it is Guattari who advances furthest toward a posthumanist understanding of the second media age social landscape. He enacts a critique of humanist positions by adopting the standpoint of "machinic heterogenesis":

> The signifying articulation . . . is unable to impose itself upon machine intensities as a relation of immanence. In other words, it cannot preside over what constitutes the nondiscursive and self-enunciating nexus of the machine. The diverse modalities of machine autopoiesis essentially escape from signifying mediation and refuse to submit to any general syntax describing the procedures of deterritorialization.[39]

Once outside the humanist strategies of Lacanian psychoanalysis, philosophies of consciousness and the rest, machine logic emerges as articulations of "multiple alterity." The principle of these "machine orderings" must be understood not as man's instrument but as a successor to human sociality.

These initiatives in conceptualizing the human–machine relation in a posthumanist age, whose outlines are only mentioned here, are the basis for a fundamental reconstruction of critical theory that will open the way to a fresh understanding of the new interactive media and the lines of resistance to them. In a most salutary way they abandon the logic of "reification" that has limited critical social theory to announcing incursions of the machine into the human, to the function of gatekeeper for the modernist subject.

One strategy to explore the social landscape so as to recognize its imbrication of human and machine is to examine the term "interface." Provisionally we may say that an interface stands between the human and the machinic, a kind of membrane dividing yet connecting two worlds that are alien to and also dependent upon each other. The interface may derive its characteristics more from the machine, as users of the DOS interface complain, or from its human side, as advocates of the Apple interface assert, or from a relatively equal portion of each.[40] The interface of earlier machines was either transparent (as with the refrigerator) or completely opaque to the uninitiated (as with machine tools). With representational machines such as the computer the question of the interface becomes especially salient because each side of the human/machine divide now begins to claim its own reality; on one side of the screen is Newtonian space, on the other, cyberspace. Interfaces of high quality allow seamless crossings between the two worlds, thereby facilitating the disappearance of the difference between them and thereby, as well, altering the type of linkage between the two. Interfaces are the sensitive boundary zone of negotiation between the human and the machinic as well as the pivot of an emerging new set of human/machine relations.

One may object to the introduction of the term "second media age." First, it incurs an absolute divide that is not warranted by distribution of media. Second, it reproduces a binary logic (first age/second age) that contains all the problems of this logic as analyzed above. Third, it maintains a stress on the technology, on the construction of the subject, losing sight of the problem of reception or resistance.

The first problem, the question of periodization, draws attention to the historical character of my analysis. I regard the work of social theory, in the spirit of Marx, as precisely the determination of the historical, of what is changing, in relation to forms of domination and potentials of freedom. In this sense critical theory is tied to the Enlightenment, or, as Foucault said, to its "spirit of critique." But periodization is an analytic gesture, not an ontologizing one. While there are certainly performative qualities to discursive acts, my introduction of "the second media age" draws rhetorical attention to certain innovations; it does not engrave lines of division in the streets of everyday life. Certainly earlier conditions continue and certainly they predominate. In the next chapter I attempt to specify the novel attributes of certain media technology so that the brunt of my case for a "new age" rests with its success. Yet the insertion of a period may suggest not a passage from one state of being to another but a complexification, a folding in of one structure upon another, a multiplying or multiplexing of different principles in the same social space. Periods or epochs do not succeed but implicate one another, do not replace but supplement one another, are not consecutive but simultaneous.

The response to the first objection leads into a response to the second. The concept of a second media age does serve as a binary to a first media age: it puts the first age into a new perspective, minimizes it perhaps, and certainly historicizes by rendering it relative or even subordinate to a second age. The second age deflates the pretensions of what now appears as a first age to having not been an age at all. Until now the broadcast model has not been a first age but has been naturalized as the only possible way of having media – few producers, many consumers. To the extent that all of this almost Oedipal conflict is implied in the notion of a second media age, then I have indeed introduced a binary. Since I am producing a discourse, one that works within the modern even if it wishes to be a critique, this should not be surprising or disappointing. The experience of feminist theory, as Teresa de Lauretis argues, suggests that efforts to escape completely dominant conditions end in reproducing them by other means: *écriture féminine* produces a foundationalism of a new kind.[41] The key issue is the awareness of the problem of the binary as one introduces new terms, not to forestall that introduction, but to render it reflexive.

The third question concerns the relative emphasis or orientation of my analysis in terms of the mechanism of subject constitution. If one works outside the binary autonomy/heteronomy, bypassing techno-logical determinism, an alternative is still open of an analytic of technologies of power: this brings into relief the discourse/practices which etch contours of identity versus an analytic of modes of appro-priation/resistance which highlight the agency of reception. The former is characteristic of poststructuralist strategies, the latter of the Birmingham school of cultural studies. I regard the two as comple-mentary. With regard to what I call the first media age – television advertisements, for example – I argue in *The Mode of Information* that the model of massification misses the process of subject construc-tion. One could also and equally study reception of TV ads as "reading," resymbolization, even resistance.[42] The difference con-cerns whether one is more interested in studying the structures of domination, in which case the first method is primary, or the ability of agents to transform their conditions, in which case the second method is more appropriate. It remains my conviction that (1) the ability of humans to change their circumstances is not in question, (2) the current situation is one of confusion about the nature of domina-tion and the character of alternatives to it, and so (3) it is most urgent to begin an analysis of conditions, or as Fredric Jameson says, a "cognitive mapping," rather than insist on the revolutionary charac-ter of agency.

2

Postmodern Virtualities

On the eve of the twenty-first century there have been two innovative discussions about the general conditions of life: one concerns a possible "postmodern" culture and even society; the other concerns broad, massive changes in communications systems. Postmodern culture is often presented as an alternative to existing society, which is pictured as structurally limited or fundamentally flawed. New communications systems are often presented as a hopeful key to a better life and a more equitable society. The discussion of postmodern culture focuses to a great extent on an emerging new individual identity or subject position, one that abandons what may in retrospect be the narrow scope of the modern individual with its claims to rationality and autonomy. The discourse surrounding the new communications systems attends more to the imminent technical increase in information exchange and the ways this advantage will redound to already existing individuals and already existing institutions. My purpose in this chapter is to bring these two discussions together, to enact a confrontation between them so that the advantages of each may redound to the other, while the limitations of each may be revealed and discarded. My contention is that a critical understanding of the new communications systems requires an evaluation of the type of subject it encourages, while a viable articulation of postmodernity must include an elaboration of its relation to new technologies of communication. Finally I shall turn to the issue of multiculturalism in relation to the postmodern subject in the age of the mode of information.

For what is at stake in these technical innovations, I contend, is not simply an increased "efficiency" of interchange, enabling new

avenues of investment, increased productivity at work and new domains of leisure and consumption, but a broad and extensive change
in the culture, in the way identities are structured. If I may be allowed
a historical analogy: the technically advanced societies are at a point
in their history similar to that of the emergence of an urban, merchant
culture in the midst of feudal society in the Middle Ages. At that point
practices of the exchange of commodities required individuals to act
and speak in new ways,[1] ways drastically different from the aristocratic code of honor with its face-to-face encounters based on trust
for one's word and its hierarchical bonds of interdependency. Interacting with total strangers sometimes at great distances, the merchants required written documents guaranteeing spoken promises
and an "arms length distance" attitude even when face to face with
the other, so as to afford a "space" for calculations of self-interest. A
new identity was constructed, gradually and in a most circuitous path
to be sure, among the merchants in which a coherent, stable sense of
individuality was grounded in independent, cognitive abilities. In this
way the cultural basis for the modern world was begun, one that
eventually would rely upon print media to encourage and disseminate
these urban forms of identity.

In the twentieth century electronic media are supporting an equally
profound transformation of cultural identity. Telephone, radio, film,
television, the computer and now their integration as "multimedia"
reconfigure words, sounds and images so as to cultivate new configurations of individuality. If modern society may be said to foster an
individual who is rational, autonomous, centered, and stable (the
"reasonable man" of the law, the educated citizen of representative
democracy, the calculating "economic man" of capitalism, the grade-
defined student of public education), then perhaps a postmodern
society is emerging which nurtures forms of identity different from,
even opposite to, those of modernity. And electronic communications
technologies significantly enhance these postmodern possibilities.
Discussions of these technologies, as we shall see, tend often to miss
precisely this crucial level of analysis, treating them as enhance-
ments for already formed individuals to deploy to their advantage or
disadvantage.[2]

I   The Communications "Superhighway"

One may regard the media from a purely technical point of view, to
the extent that it is possible, evaluating them in relation to their

ability to transmit units of information. The question to ask, then, is how much information with how little noise may be transmitted at what speed and over what distance to how many locations? Until the late 1980s technical constraints limited the media's ability in these terms. To transmit a high quality image over existing (twisted pair copper wire) phone lines took about ten minutes using a 2,400 baud modem or two minutes using a 9,600 baud modem. Given these specifications it was not possible to send "real time" "moving" images over the phone lines. The great limitation then of the first electronic media age is that images could only be transmitted from a small number of centers to a large number of receivers, either by air or by coaxial cable. Until the end of the 1980s an "economic" scarcity existed in the media highways that encouraged and justified, without much thought or consideration, the capitalist or nation-state exploitation of image transmission. Since senders needed to build their own information roads by broadcasting at a given frequency or by constructing (coaxial) wire networks, there were necessarily few distributors of images. The same economies of technology, it might be noted in passing, applied to processes of information production.

Critical theorists such as Benjamin, Enzensberger and McLuhan[3] envisioned the democratic potential of the increased communication capacity of radio, film and television. While there is some truth to their position, the practical model for a more radical communications potential during the first media age was rather the telephone. What distinguishes the telephone from the other great media is its decentralized quality and its universal exchangeability of the positions of sender and receiver. Anyone can "produce" and send a message to anyone else in the system and, in the advanced industrial societies, almost everyone is in the system. These unique qualities were recognized early on by both defenders and detractors of the telephone.

In the recent past the only technology that imitates the telephone's democratic structure is the Internet, the government-funded electronic mail, database and general communication system.[4] Until the 1990s, even this facility had been restricted largely to government, research and education institutions and some private industry and individuals who enroll in private services (Compuserve, Prodigy) which are connected to it. In the last few years Internet has gained enormously in popularity and by the mid-1990s boasts thirty million users around the world.[5] But Internet and its segments use the phone lines, suffering their inherent technical limitations. Technical innovations in the late 1980s and early 1990s, however, are making possible the drastic reduction of earlier constraints. The digital encoding of sound, text and image, the introduction of fiber optic lines replacing copper wire, the ability to transmit digitally encoded images and the subsequent ability to compress this information, the vast expansion of the frequency range for wireless transmission, innovations in switching technology, and a number of other advances have so enlarged the quantity and types of information that may soon be able to be transmitted that a qualitative change, to allude to Engels's dialectical formula, in the culture may also be imminent.

Information superhighways are being constructed that will enable a vast increase in the flow of communications. The telephone and cable companies are estimating the change to be from a limit of sixty or so one-way video/audio channels to one of five hundred with limited bidirectionality. But this kind of calculation badly misses the point. The increase in transmission capacity (both wired and wireless) will be so great that it will be possible to transmit any type of information (audio, video or text) from any point in the network to any other point or points, and to do so in "real time," in other words quickly enough so that the receiver will see or record at least 24 frames of video per second with an accompanying audio frequency range of twenty to twenty thousand Hertz. The metaphor of the "superhighway" attends only to the movement of information, leaving out the various kinds of cyber*space* on the Internet, meeting places, work areas, and electronic cafes in which this vast transmission of images and words becomes places of communicative relation. The question that needs to be raised is "will this technological change provide the stimulus for the installation of new media different enough from what we now have to warrant the periodizing judgment of a second electronic media age?" If that is the case, how is the change to be understood?

A discourse on the new communications technology is in process of formation, one which is limited largely by the vision of modernity. The importance of the information superhighway is now widely recognized, with articles appearing in periodicals from the specialized zines (*Wired* and *Mondo 2,000*) to general journals (*Time, Forbes* and *The Nation*). Essays on the new technology vary from breathless enthusiasm to wary caution to skepticism. Writing in *Time*, Philip Elmer-Dewitt forecasts: "The same switches used to send a TV show to your home can also be used to send a video from your home to any other – paving the way for video phones . . . The same system will allow anybody with a camcorder to distribute videos to the world . . ."[6] Key to the new media system is not only the technical advances mentioned above but also the merger of existing communication technologies. Elmer-Dewitt continues, ". . . the new technology will force the merger of television, telecommunications, computers, consumer electronics, publishing and information services into a single interactive information industry" (pp. 52–3). Other observers emphasize the prospects of wireless technology. Writing in *Forbes*, George Gilder predicts the spread of this system: ". . . the new minicell replaces a rigid structure of giant analog mainframes with a system of wireless local area networks . . . these wide and weak [replacing broadcasting based on "long and strong"] radios can handle voice, data and even video at the same time . . . the system fulfills the promise of the computer revolution as a spectrum multiplier . . . [the new system will] banish once and for all the concept of spectrum scarcity . . ."[7] Whether future communications media employ wired, wireless or some combination of the two, the same picture emerges of profound transformation.

Faced with this gigantic combination of new technology, integration of older technologies, creation of new industries and expansion of older ones, commentators have not missed the political implications. In *Tikkun*, David Bollier underlines the need for a new set of policies to govern and regulate the second media age in the public interest. President Bill Clinton and Vice-President Al Gore have already drawn attention to the problem, stressing the need for broad access to the superhighway, but also indicating their willingness to make the new developments safe for the profit motive. For them the main issue at stake is the strength of the United States in relation to other nations (read especially Japan) and the health of the industries involved. Bollier points to wider concerns, such as strengthening community life, supporting families and invigorating the democratic process.[8] At this point I want to note that Bollier understands the new media entirely within the framework of *modern* social institutions. The "information superhighway" is for him a transparent tool that brings new efficiencies but by itself changes nothing. The media merely redound to the benefit of or detract from familiar institutions – the family, the community, the state.

If Bollier presents a liberal or left-liberal agenda for politics confronted by the second media age, Mitchell Kapor, former developer of Lotus 1-2-3, offers a more radical interpretation. He understands better than Bollier that the information superhighway opens qualitatively new political opportunities because it creates new loci of speech: ". . . the crucial political question is 'Who controls the switches?' There are two extreme choices. Users may have indirect, or limited control over when, what, why, and from whom they get information and to whom they send it. That's the broadcast model today, and it seems to breed consumerism, passivity, crassness, and mediocrity. Or, users may have decentralized, distributed, direct control over when, what, why, and with whom they exchange information. That's the Internet model today, and it seems to breed critical thinking, activism, democracy, and quality. We have an opportunity to choose now."[9] With Kapor, the interpretation of the new media returns to the position of Enzensberger: socialist or radical democratic control of the media results in more freedom, more enlightenment, more rationality; capitalist or centralist control results in oppression, passivity, irrationality. Kapor's reading of the information superhighway remains within the binaries of modernity. No new cultural formations of the self are imagined or even thought possible. While the political questions raised by Bollier and Kapor are valid and raise the level of debate well beyond its current formation, they remain limited to the terms of discussion that are familiar in the landscape of modernity.

The political implications of the Internet for the fate of the nation-state and the development of a global community also require attention. The dominant use of English on the Internet suggests the extension of American power, as does the fact that e-mail addresses in the United States alone do not require a country code. The Internet normalizes American users. But the issue is more complex. In Singapore, English serves to *enable* conversations between hostile ethnic groups, being a neutral "other." Of course, vast inequalities of use exist, changing the democratic structure of the Internet into an occasion for further wrongs to the poorer populations. Even within the high-use nations, wealthy white males are disproportionate users. Yet technologies sometimes spread quickly and the Internet is relatively cheap. Only grassroots political mobilization on this issue will ensure wide access.[10]

In some ways the Internet undermines the territoriality of the nation-state: messages in cyberspace are not easily delimited in Newtonian space, rendering borders ineffective. In the Teale–Homolka trial of early 1994, a case of multiple murders including sexual assault and mutilation, the Canadian government was unable to enforce an information blackout because of Usenet postings in the United States being available in Canada.[11] In order to combat communicative acts that are defined by one state as illegal, nations are being compelled to coordinate their laws, putting their vaunted "sovereignty" in question. So desperate are national governments, confronted by the disorder of the Internet, that schemes to monitor all messages are afoot, such as the American government's idea to monopolize encryption with a "Clipper Chip" or the FBI's insistence on building surveillance mechanisms into the structure of the information superhighway.[12] Nation-states are at a loss when faced with a global communication network. Technology has taken a turn that defies the character of power of modern governments.

The effortless reproduction and distribution of information is greeted by modern economic organizations, the corporations, with the same anxiety that plagues nation-states. Audio taping was resisted by the moguls of the music industry; video taping by Hollywood; modems by the telephone industry giants. Property rights are put in doubt when information is set free of its material integument to move and to multiply in cyberspace with few constraints. The response of our captains of industry is the absurd one of attempting vastly to extend the principle of property by promulgating new "intellectual property laws," flying in the face of the advance in the technologies of transmission and dissemination. The problem for capitalism is how to contain the word and the image, to bind them to proper names and logos when they flit about at the speed of light and procreate with indecent rapidity, not arborially, to use the terms of Deleuze and Guattari, as in a centralized factory, but rhyzomically, at any decentered location. If that were not enough to daunt defenders of modern notions of property, First Amendment issues are equally at risk. Who, for example, "owns" the rights to and is thereby responsible for the text on Internet bulletin boards: the author, the system operator, the community of participants? Does freedom of speech extend to cyberspace, as it does to print? How easy will it be to assess damages and mete out blame in a communicative world whose contours are quite different from those of face-to-face speech and print? These and numerous other fundamental questions are raised by Internet communications for institutions, laws and habits that developed in the very different context of modernity.

II Reality Problematized

Before turning to the issue of the cultural interpretation of the second media age, we need to consider a further new technology, that of virtual reality. The term "virtual" was used in computer jargon to refer to situations that were near substitutes. For example, virtual memory means the use of a section of a hard disk to act as something else, in this case, random access memory. "Virtual reality" is a more dangerous term since it suggests that reality may be multiple or take many forms.[13] The phrase is close to that of "real time," which arose in the audio recording field when splicing, multiple-track recording and multiple-speed recording made possible "other times" to that of clock time or phenomenological time. In this case, the normal or conventional sense of "time" had to be preserved by the modifier "real." But again the use of the modifier only draws attention to non-"reality" of clock time, its non-exclusivity, its insubstantiality, its lack of foundation. The terms "virtual reality" and "real time" attest to the force of the second media age in constituting a simulational culture. The mediation has become so intense that the things mediated can no longer even pretend to be unaffected. The culture is increasingly simulational in the sense that the media often changes the things that it treats, transforming the identity of originals and referentialities. In the second media age "reality" becomes multiple.

Virtual reality is a computer-generated "place" which is "viewed" by the participant through "goggles" but which responds to stimuli from the participant or participants. A participant may "walk" through a house that is being designed for him or her to get a feel for it before it is built. Or s/he may "walk" through a "museum" or "city" whose paintings or streets are computer-generated but the position of the individual is relative to their actual movement, not to a predetermined computer program or "movie." In addition, more than one individual may experience the same virtual reality at the same time, with both persons' "movements" affecting the same "space." What is more, these individuals need not be in the same physical location but may be communicating information to the computer from distant points through modems. Further "movements" in virtual reality are not quite the same as movements in "old reality": for example, one can fly or go through walls since the material constraints of earth need not apply. While still in their infancy, virtual reality programs attest to the increasing "duplication," if I may use this term, of reality by technology. But the duplication incurs an alternation: virtual realities are fanciful imaginings that, in their difference from real reality, evoke play and discovery, instituting a new level of imagination. Virtual reality takes the imaginary of the word and the imaginary of the film or video image one step further by placing the individual "inside" alternative worlds. By directly tinkering with reality, a simulational practice is set in place which alters forever the conditions under which the identity of the self is formed.

Already transitional forms of virtual reality are in use on the Internet. MUDs or Multi User Domains have a devoted following. These are conferences of sorts in which participants adopt roles in a neo-medieval adventure game. Although the game is played textually, that is, moves are typed as sentences, it is highly "visual" in the sense that complex locations, characters and objects interact continuously. In a variant of a MUD, LambdaMOO, a database contains "objects" as "built" by participants to improve upon the sense of reality. As a result, a quasi-virtual reality is created by the players. What is more, each player adopts a fictional role that may be different from their actual gender and indeed this gender may change in the course of the game, drastically calling into question the gender system of the dominant culture as a fixed binary. At least during the fictional game, individuals explore imaginary subject positions while in communication with others. In LambdaMOO, a series of violent "rapes" by one character caused a crisis among the participants, one that led to special conferences devoted to the issue of punishing the offender and thereby better defining the nature of the community space of the conference. This experience also cautions against depictions of cyberspace as utopia: the wounds of modernity are borne with us when we enter this new arena and in some cases are even exacerbated. Nonetheless, the makings of a new cultural space are also at work in the MUDs. One player argues that continuous participation in the game leads to a sense of involvement that is somewhere between ordinary reality and fiction.[14] The effect of new media such as the Internet and virtual reality, then, is to multiply the kinds of "realities" one encounters in society.

III The Postmodern Subject

The information superhighway and virtual reality are communications media that enrich existing forms of consumer culture. But they also depart or may depart from what we have known as the mass media or the "culture industry" in a number of crucial ways. I said "may depart" because neither of these technologies has been fully constituted as a cultural practice; they are emergent communication systems whose features are yet to be specified with some permanence of finality. One purpose of this chapter is to suggest the importance of some form of political concern about how these technologies are being actualized. The technical characteristics of the information superhighway and virtual reality are clear enough to call attention to their potential for new cultural formations. It is conceivable that the information superhighway will be restricted in the way the broadcast system is. In that case, the term "second media age" is unjustified. But the potential of a decentralized communications system is so great that it is certainly worthy of recognition.

Examples from the history of the installation and dissemination of communications technologies are instructive. Carolyn Marvin points out that the telephone was, at the onset, by no means the universal, decentralized network it became. The phone company was happy to restrict the use of the instrument to those who registered. It did not understand the social or political importance of the universality of participation, being interested mainly in income from services provided. Also the example of Telefon Hirmondó, a telephone system in Budapest in the period before World War I, is worth recalling. The Hungarians used the telephone as a broadcast system, with a published schedule of programming. They also restricted narrowly the dissemination of the technology to the ruling class. The process by which the telephone was instituted as a universally disseminated network in which anyone is able to call anyone else occurred in a complex, multi-leveled historical articulation in which the technology, the economic structure, the political institution, the political culture and the mass of the population each played interacting roles.[15] A similarly complex history will no doubt accompany the institution of the information superhighway and virtual reality.

In *The Mode of Information* I argued that electronic communications constitute the subject in ways other than that of the major modern institutions. If modernity or the mode of production signifies patterned practices that elicit identities as autonomous and (instrumentally) rational, postmodernity or the mode of information indicates communication practices that constitute subjects as unstable, multiple and diffuse. The information superhighway and virtual reality will extend the mode of information to still further applications, greatly amplifying its diffusion by bringing more practices and more individuals within its pattern of formation. No doubt many modern institutions and practices continue to exist and indeed dominate social space. The mode of information is an emergent phenomenon that affects small but important aspects of everyday life. It certainly does not blanket the advanced industrial societies and has even less presence in less developed nations. The information superhighway and virtual reality may be interpreted through the poststructuralist lens I have used here in relation to the cultural issue of subject constitution. If that is done, the question of the mass media is seen not simply as that of sender/receiver, producer/consumer, ruler/ruled. The shift to a decentralized network of communications makes senders receivers, producers consumers, rulers ruled, upsetting the logic of understanding of the first media age. The step I am suggesting is at least temporarily to abandon that logic and adopt a poststructuralist cultural analysis of modes of subject constitution. This does not answer all the questions opened by the second media age, especially the political ones which at the moment are extremely difficult. But it permits the recognition of an emergent postmodernity and a tentative approach to a political analysis of *that* cultural system; it allows the beginning of a line of thought that confronts the possibility of a new age, avoiding the continued, limiting exclusive repetition of the logics of modernity.

Subject constitution in the second media age occurs through the mechanism of interactivity. A technical term referring to two-way communications, "interactivity" has become, by dint of the advertising campaigns of telecommunications corporations, desirable as an end in itself, so that its usage can float and be applied in countless contexts having little to do with telecommunications. Yet the phenomenon of communicating at a distance through one's computer, of sending and receiving digitally encoded messages, of being "interactive" has been the most popular application of the Internet. Far more than making purchases or obtaining information electronically, communicating by computer claims the intense interest of countless thousands.[16] The use of the Internet to simulate communities far outstrips its function as retail store or reference work. In the words of Howard Rheingold, an enthusiastic Internet user, "I can attest that I and thousands of other cybernauts know that what we are looking for, and finding in some surprising ways, is not just information but instant access to ongoing relationships with a large number of other people."[17] Rheingold terms the network of relations that come into existence on Internet bulletin boards "virtual communities." Places for "meeting" on the Internet, such as "the Well" frequented by Rheingold, provide "areas" for "public" messages, which all subscribers may read, and private "mailbox" services for individual exchanges.

The understanding of these communications is limited by modern categories of analysis. For example, many have interpreted the success of "virtual communities" as an indication that "real" communities are in decline. Internet provides an alternative, these critics contend, to the real thing.[18] But the opposition "virtual" and "real" community contains serious difficulties. In the case of the nation, generally regarded as the strongest group identification in the modern period and thus perhaps the most "real" community of this era, the role of the imaginary has been fundamental.[19] Pre-electronic media, like the newspaper, were instrumental in disseminating the sign of the nation and interpellating the subject in relation to it. In even earlier types of community, such as the village, kinship and residence were salient factors of determination. But identification of an individual or family with a specific group was never automatic, natural or given, always turning, as Jean-Luc Nancy argues, on the production of an "essence" which reduces multiplicity into fixity, obscuring the political process in which "community" is constructed: ". . . the thinking of community as essence . . . is in effect the closure of the political."[20] He rephrases the term community by asking the following question: "How can we be receptive to the *meaning* of our multiple, dispersed, mortally fragmented existences, which nonetheless only make sense by existing in common?" (p. xl). Community for him, then, is paradoxically the absence of "community." It is rather the matrix of fragmented identities, each pointing toward the other, which he chooses to term "writing."

Nancy's critique of community in the older sense is crucial to the understanding of the construction of self in the Internet. For his part Nancy has chosen to deny the significance of new communications technologies, as well as new subaltern subject positions in his understanding of community: "The emergence and our increasing consciousness of decolonized communities has not profoundly modified [the givens of community], nor has today's growth of unprecedented forms of being-in-common – through channels of information as well as through what is called the 'multiracial society' – triggered any genuine renewal of the question of community" (p. 22). Nancy denies the relation I am drawing between a postmodern constitution of the subject and bidirectional communications media. The important point, however, is that in order to do so he first posits the subject as "multiple, dispersed, mortally fragmented" in an ontological statement. To this extent he removes the question of community from the arena of history and politics, the exact purpose of his critique of the essentialist community in the first place. While presenting an effective critique of the essentialist community, Nancy reinstates the problem at the level of the subject by ontologizing its *in*essentialism. My preference is rather to specify the historical emergence of the decentered subject and explore its links with new communications situations.

We may now return to the question of the Internet and its relation to a "virtual community." To restate the issue: the Internet and virtual reality open the possibility of new kinds of interactivity such that the idea of an opposition of real and unreal community is not adequate to specify the differences between modes of bonding, serving instead to obscure the manner of the historical construction of forms of community. In particular this opposition prevents asking the question of the forms of identity prevalent in various types of community. The notion of a real community, as Nancy shows, presupposes the fixed, stable identities of its members, the exact assumption that Internet communities put into question. Observers of and participants in Internet "virtual communities" repeat in near unanimity that long or intense experience with computer-mediated electronic communication is associated with a certain fluidity of identity. Rheingold foresees huge cultural changes as the effect of Internet use on the individual: ". . . are relationships and commitments as we know them even possible in a place where identities are fluid? . . . We reduce and encode our identities as words on a screen, decode and unpack the identities of others" (p. 61). In bulletin boards such as the Well, people connect with strangers without much of the social baggage that divides and alienates. Without visual cues about gender, age, ethnicity and social status, conversations open up in directions that otherwise might be avoided. Participants in these virtual communities often express themselves with little inhibition and dialogues flourish and develop quickly. Yet Rheingold attributes the conviviality of the Well and the extravagant identity transformations of MUDs to "the hunger for community that has followed the disintegration of traditional communities around the world" (p. 62). Even for this advocate of new communications technologies, the concept of a real community regulates his understanding of the new interactivity. While there may be some truth to a perspective that sees "virtual communities" as compensations for the loss of real communities, I prefer to explore the new territory and define its possibilities.

Another aspect to understanding identity in virtual communities is provided by Stone. Her studies of electronic communication systems suggest that participants code "virtual" reality through categories of "normal" reality. They do so by communicating to each other as if they were in physical common space, as if this space were inhabited by bodies, were mappable by Cartesian perspective, and by regarding the interactions as events, as fully significant for the participants' personal histories.[21] While treatment of new media by categories developed in relation to earlier ones is hardly new, in this case the overlap serves to draw closer together the two types of ontological status. Virtual communities derive some of their verisimilitude from being treated as if they were plain communities, allowing members to experience communications in cyberspace as if they were embodied social interactions. Just as virtual communities are understood as having the attributes of "real" communities, so "real" communities can be seen to depend on the imaginary: what makes a community vital to its members is their treatment of the communications as meaningful and important. Virtual and real communities mirror each other in chiasmic juxtaposition.

IV   Narratives in Cyberspace

Electronic mail services and bulletin boards are inundated by stories. Individuals appear to enjoy relating narratives to those they have never met and probably never will meet. These narratives often seem to emerge directly from people's lives but many no doubt are inventions. The appeal is strong to tell one's tale to others – to many, many others. One observer suggests the novelty of the situation: "technology is breaking down the notion of few-to-many communications. Some communicators will always be more powerful than others, but the big idea behind cyber-tales is that for the first time the many are talking to the many. Every day, those who can afford the computer equipment and the telephone bills can be their own producers, agents, editors and audiences. Their stories are becoming more and more idiosyncratic, interactive and individualistic, told in different forums to diverse audiences in different ways."[22] This explosion of narrativity depends upon a technology that is unlike print and unlike the electronic media of the first age: it is cheap, flexible, readily available, quick. It combines the decentralized model of the telephone and its numerous "producers" of messages with the broadcast model's advantage of numerous receivers. Audio (Internet Talk Radio) and video (The World-Wide Web using Mosaic) are being added to text, enhancing considerably the potentials of the new narratives. There is now a "World-Wide Web" which allows the simultaneous transmission of text, images and sound, providing hypertext links as well. The implications of the Web are astounding: film clips and voice readings may be included in "texts" and "authors" may indicate their links as "texts." In addition, other related technologies produce similar decentralizing effects. Such phenomena as "desktop broadcasting," widespread citizen camcorder "reporting" and digital filmmaking are transgressing the constraints of broadcast oligopolies.[23]

The question of narrative position has been central to the discussion of postmodernity. Jean-François Lyotard has analyzed the change in narrative legitimation structures of the premodern, modern and postmodern epochs. Lyotard defines the postmodern as an "incredulity" toward metanarratives, especially that of progress and its variants deriving from the Enlightenment.[24] He advocates a turn to the "little story," which validates difference, extols the "unpresentable" and escapes the overbearing logic of instrumentality that derives from the metanarrative of progress. Any effort to relate second media age technologies with the concept of the postmodern must confront Lyotard's skepticism about technology. For Lyotard, it must be recalled, technology itself is fully complicit with *modern* narrativity. For example, he warns of the dangers of "a generalized computerization of society" in which the availability of knowledge is politically dangerous: "The performativity of an utterance ... increases proportionally to the amount of information about its referent one has at one's disposal. Thus the growth of power, and its self-legitimation, are now taking the route of data storage and accessibility, and the operativity of information" (p. 47). Information technologies are thus complicit with new tendencies toward totalitarian control, not toward a decentralized, multiple "little narrativity" of postmodern culture.

The question may be raised, then, of the narrative structure of second media age communications: does it or is it likely to promote the proliferation of little narratives or does it invigorate a developing authoritarian technocracy? Lyotard describes the narrative structure of tribal, premodern society as stories that (1) legitimate institutions, (2) contain many different forms of language, (3) are transmitted by senders who are part of the narrative and have heard it before and

listeners who are possible senders, (4) construct a non-linear temporality that foreshortens the past and the present, rendering each
repetition of the story strangely concurrent, and, most importantly,
(5) authorize everyone as a narrator. Modern society, Lyotard argues,
derives its legitimacy from narratives about science. Within science
language (1) does not legitimate institutions, (2) contains the single
language form of denotation, (3) does not confirm addressee as
possible sender, (4) gains no validity by being reported, and (5)
constructs "diachronic" temporality. These contrasting characteristics may serve, as Lyotard wishes, to indicate the "pragmatics" of
language. It would be interesting to analyze the role of technologies in
the premodern and modern cases, and especially the change, within
the modern, from print to broadcast media.

In any case, for Lyotard, the postmodern little narrative
refunctions the premodern language game, but only in limited ways.
Like the tribal myth, the little narrative insists on "the het-
eromorphous nature of language games" (p. 66); in short, it validates difference. Unlike older narrative forms, the little narrative
emphasizes the role of invention, the indication of the unknown and
the unexpected. Lyotard looks to certain developments in the natural
sciences for his examples of such postmodern narratives, but we may
turn to the Internet and to the developing technology of virtual
reality. As we have seen, the Internet seems to encourage the proliferation of stories, local narratives without any totalizing gestures, and
it places senders and addressees in symmetrical relations. Moreover
these stories and their performance consolidate the "social bond" of
the Internet "community," much like the premodern narrative. But
invention is central to the Internet, especially in MUDs and virtual
reality: the production of the unknown or paralogy, in Lyotard's
term, is central to second media age communications. In particular
the relation of the utterance to representation is not limited to denotation as in the modern language game of science, and indeed the
technology encourages a lightening of the weight of the referent. This
is an important basis for the instability of identity in electronic
communications, leading to the insertion of the question of the subject and its construction. In this spirit, Katherine Hayles defines the
"revolutionary potential" of virtual reality as follows: "to expose the
presuppositions underlying the social formations of late capitalism
and to open new fields of play where the dynamics have not yet
rigidified and new kinds of moves are possible."[25]

For the new technologies install the "interface," the face between
the faces; the face that insists that we remember that we have "faces,"

that we have sides that are present at the moment of utterance, that we are not present in any simple or immediate way. The interface has become critical to the success of the Internet. To attain wide appeal, the Internet must not simply be efficient, useful or entertaining: it must present itself in an agreeable manner. The enormous problem for interface design is the fear and hostility humans nourish toward machines and toward a dim recognition of a changing relation toward them, a sharing of space and an interdependence.[26] The Internet interface must somehow appear "transparent," that is to say, appear not to be an interface, not to come between two alien beings, and also seem fascinating, announcing its novelty and encouraging an exploration of the difference of the machinic. The problem of the Internet, then, is not simply "technological" but para-machinic: to construct a boundary between the human and the machinic that draws the human into the technology, transforming the technology into "used equipment" and the human into a "cyborg," into one meshing with machines.[27]

In Wim Wenders's recent film "Until the End of the World" (1991), several characters view their own dreams on videotape, becoming so absorbed in what they see that they forget to eat and sleep. The characters sit transfixed before their viewing devices, ignoring everyone around them, disregarding all relations and affairs. Limited to the micro-world of their own dreams the characters are lost in a narcissistic stupor. And yet their total absorption is compelling. Visual representations of the unconscious – no doubt Wenders has film itself in mind – are irresistible compared to everyday reality, a kind of hyper-reality.

One can imagine that virtual reality devices will become as compelling as the dream videos in Wenders's film. Virtual reality machines should be able to allow the participant to enter imagined worlds with convincing verisimilitude, releasing immense potentials for fantasy, self-discovery and self-construction. When groups of individuals are able to interact in the same virtual space, the possibilities are even more difficult to conceive. One hesitates to suggest that these experiences are commensurate with something that has been termed community. Yet there is every reason to think that virtual reality technologies will develop rapidly and will eventually enable participation through the Internet. Connected to one's home computer, one will experience an audiovisual "world" generated from a node somewhere in the Internet, and this will include other participants in the same way that today one can communicate with others on bulletin boards in videotext. If such experiences become commonplace, just as viewing television is today, then surely reality will have been multiplied. The continued Western quest for making tools may at that point retrospectively be reinterpreted in relation to its culmination in virtual reality. From the club that extends and replaces the arm to virtual reality in cyberspace, technology has evolved to mime and to multiply, to multiplex and to improve upon the real.

V   Multiculturalism and the Postmodern Media Age

If the second media age constitutes subjects in a postmodern pattern, critics have ascribed similarities between the politics of multiculturalism and the culture of postmodernity. Political positions surrounding issues of ethnicity and race are various and complex. But commentators have noted a filiation between Lyotard's critique of pluralism in favor of the differend and the multiculturalists' parallel attack on liberal pluralism. In this connection, two questions are paramount: (1) what is the relation of the second media age to ethnicity? and (2) what is the relation between the multiculturalist critique of modernity and the challenge to it by the second media age?

In many respects, the dissemination of second media age communications systems is likely to dispense with the question of ethnicity with the same disregard as has the first media age. In the absence of an effective anti-racist political movement, dominant institutions tend to be constructed as if white were the only race, Anglo-Saxon the only ethnicity and Christianity the only religion. Participation in the information superhighway and virtual reality will most likely be accessible to and culturally consonant with wealthy, white males. In these respects the media reflect the relations of force that prevail in the wider community. At another level, one may ask if these media intrinsically favor one group over another. Is virtual reality, for example, somehow white or somehow masculine? I believe these questions are important to raise but that they cannot be answered at present beyond a few brief remarks. The new technologies, even after two decades of the new social movements, are likely to have been conceived, designed and produced by white males. In that respect they are likely to conform at some level to the cultural peculiarities of that group. The best example of this may be found in video games. Beyond this uncomfortably vague statement, one cannot at present say much more. The technoculture of the second media age largely remains to be constructed.

With respect to the second question – the relation of multiculturalist and second media age resistances to the modern – there is more to be said. Multiculturalists claim some affinity with critiques of the modern that depart from the poststructuralist rejection of the Enlightenment view of the subject. The rational, autonomous individual who pre-exists society, as Descartes and Locke maintained, emerges after the critique by poststructuralists as a Western cultural figure associated with specific groups and practices, not as the unquestioned embodiment of some universal. One may argue that such attributes ought to be desired or realized by everyone. But then that argument is one among others and has no presumptive claims to priority over any other figuration of the subject. Multiculturalists also desire to relativize Western values, to remove the patina of universalism from what is no more than another ethnocentrism. In such critiques I can see no important difference in the poststructuralist and multiculturalist positions, both of which can be coordinated with the type of non-modernist subjects constituted by the new media.

Multiculturalists, postcolonialists and subaltern theorists sometimes further claim certain privileges for the subject position of the "minority" or "third world person" not simply as that of the oppressed but as affirming the ethnic characteristics of the group. In my view such cultural politics are not critical of the modernist position but simply shift the values or relative worth of two terms in the binary opposition autonomous rational universal/particularist non-rational other. To the extent that placing value on ethnicity promotes a recentering of the subject and supports the foundationalism or essentialism of the group in question, then the subject position so articulated has little to do with postmodernity or the second media age.[28] In "On the Jewish Question," Marx long ago effectively analyzed the limitations of such special pleading for an anti-authoritarian politics.[29] For the chief characteristics of the resistance of the new media to modernity lie in their complication of subjecthood, their denaturalizing the process of subject formation, their putting into question the interiority of the subject and its coherence. I believe these traits of the postmodern may contribute to a critique of the modern, may help to undermine the fundamental cultural configuration of modernity, whereas the type of multiculturalism that celebrates a particular ethnicity does not achieve that end. These hopeful possibilities are by no means guaranteed by the dissemination of second media age technologies and the articulation of a commensurate cultural formation.

Proponents of multiculturalism sometimes claim that post-structural theory and concepts of postmodern culture systematically limit the understanding of non-Western ethnicity by configuring it as the Other. While the "post" theories may be effective in a cultural critique of Western logocentrism, they argue, such a critique runs aground to the extent that Western identity is bound up with non-Western identity both at the levels of imperialist politics and economics as well as in the cultural domain. No doubt this argument effectively indicates a limitation of poststructuralism, one which postcolonial discourse may contribute to correcting. Indeed interpretations of ethnicity often go far in this direction, such as Rey Chow's formulation: "Ethnicity signifies the social experience which is not completed once and for all but which is constituted by a continual, often conflictual, working-out of its grounds" (p. 143). In this case multiculturalism is a process of subject constitution, not an affirmation of an essence. As the second media age unfolds and permeates everyday practice, one political issue will be the construction of new combinations of technology with multiple genders and ethnicities. These technocultures will hopefully be no return to an origin, no new foundationalism or essentialism, but a coming to terms with the process of identity constitution and doing so in ways that struggle against restrictions of systematic inequalities, hierarchies and asymmetries.

The relation of the second media age to multiculturalism is likely, then, to be profoundly ambivalent: to some extent both contribute to a critique of modernity and therefore to the dominant forms of oppression; on the other hand the new media will no doubt work against the solidification of ethnic identity and, it would appear to me, that traditionalists in the multiculturalist camp are unlikely to look with favor on the information superhighway and virtual reality. As these technologies emerge in social space the great political question will be what forms of cultural articulation they promote and discourage. One needs to keep in mind the enormous variability of the technology rather than assume its determining powers. The example of contemporary Singapore, where a policy implementing advanced information technologies is promulgated by an authoritarian regime, should serve as a warning against overly sanguine expectations.

3

Postmodernity and the Politics of Multiculturalism

Remarkable changes are taking place in the European social and political order concerning East European socialism, the demise of the Soviet Union, the political, economic, and cultural unification in Western Europe, the emergence of ecology as a political question, the transformation of "private sphere" issues into public concerns, the question of postmodern culture, the impact of advanced technologies on everyday life, and the secular trend toward a general globalization of the economy and cosmopolitanization of identities. In this context, social theory is faced with a staggering task of reconceptualization, of treating themes that challenge and stretch the viability of traditional orientations, those of Locke, Mill, Marx, Weber and Durkheim. Within the framework of an emerging new politics, a stunning controversy between Jürgen Habermas and French poststructuralists has dominated the arena of social theory since the late 1970s.

Despite the acrimony that has characterized the controversy, one fundamental issue unites the protagonists: all agree that social theory must give new priority to language. In *The Postmodern Condition* Lyotard spoke of language as basic to the social bond, in part as a consequence of the dissemination of computer technologies.[1] Similarly, Habermas in *The Philosophical Discourse of Modernity* urged a turn to language in social theory.[2] Earlier orientations on society as an arena of actions and a structure of institutions are replaced by a focus on the symbolic level. Lyotard defines the current "postmodern" age as "incredulity toward metanarratives," by which he means the inability of our intellectual heritage to make sense of our present circumstances. In a similar vein, Habermas declares "The paradigm of the philosophy of consciousness is exhausted" and urges a shift to "the paradigm of mutual understanding."[3]

Despite this convergence of tendencies, the differences between the positions far outweigh the similarities. The issues that divide Habermas and French poststructuralists may be gauged by looking at the degree of viability each is willing to accord to past theoretical frameworks in the present conjuncture and the concomitant need each position senses for new theoretical departures. In general French theorists regard the Western intellectual tradition as an obstacle to understanding the present, or more accurately as a discursive structure of domination rather than a basis for a new critical standpoint, while Habermas views their point of departure as a fall into irrationalism. Habermas attempts a reconstruction of historical materialism and aspires to the completion of the Enlightenment project of emancipation. Lyotard, Foucault, Derrida and other related French theorists signal "incredulity toward the metanarratives of emancipation," predict the demise of humanism and call for the deconstruction of the Western philosophical tradition. In the one case there is an effort to revise and conserve; in the other an urge to break out in new directions.

This divergence of views has in many cases been acrimonious: Habermas regards Derrida, Lyotard, Foucault and the rest as "Young Conservatives," and Manfred Frank, more disparagingly, characterizes Lyotard as a "neo-fascist."[4] Lyotard for his part has been equally forthcoming: the perspective of Habermas's communicative rationality is "terrorist."[5] Advocates of Habermas's position, such as Seyla Benhabib, dismiss Lyotard as "liberal pluralist" or "quietist."[6] While from outside these camps, especially in the United States, it may appear that Habermas and the poststructuralists have much in common and together constitute the main hopes for a renewal of critical social theory, the participants are not at all as sanguine, viewing each other rather as a chief enemy than a potential ally. The single hiatus within the general enmity is Habermas's short memorial essay on Foucault's death, where a somewhat promising picture of Foucault's work is given.[7]

Habermas diagnoses the present conjuncture as a mixture of serious dangers with some hope. The dangers come from the intrusion of "the system" into "the lifeworld."[8] Habermas accepts the Weberian, Lukácsian critique of modern social institutions as one of increasing differentiation of functions but also of generalized instrumentality. While the system of modern society becomes ever more complex as an

articulation of specialization, its mode of practice, instrumental rationality, is homogeneous. In the corporation, the state, the military and
the schools, the process of reification, of treating human beings as
things to be used efficiently for one's own ends, steadily extends the
domain of its sway. Outside this system stands the lifeworld, the
domain of the everyday where symbolic exchange operates according
to a non-instrumental principle. In the lifeworld communicative action is based on a different principle of rationality.[9] Symbols are
exchanged without the imperatives of the system for profit, control,
efficiency. Hence the opportunity for a critical use of reason in
communication is possible.

The lifeworld, for Habermas, is the seed bed for the growth of
emancipatory language use and action. All language, he thinks, contains the potential for a free society since it embodies, as a "universal
pragmatic," the validity claims of truth, justice and beauty. Communicative action contains a kind of rationality in that one may presuppose that speakers intend the truth, mean to express themselves and
are motivated by norms of justice. Even if these conditions are never
met in practice, Habermas posits an "ideal speech situation" in which
they may occur, a situation in which the force of the better argument
alone, not social position or coercion in any form, may prevail. When
these conditions are fulfilled social interactions are governed by the
autonomous, critical use of freedom by each participant.

But Habermas goes further. The ideal speech situation contains the
telos of consensus. The fundamental rule of communicative rationality is that the parties attempt to reach agreement; their differences are
erased in an attempt to attain unity of mind and purpose. Habermas
posits the sign of consensus as a universal, necessary principle of all
speech. The true conditions of emancipated society are fulfilled when
the universal pragmatics of speech are instituted formally as a public
sphere that aims at consensus. With the notions of consensus and the
public sphere Habermas puts forth a vision of the completion of
Enlightenment rationality, setting this in opposition to the system
rationality of liberals such as Niklaus Luhmann who content themselves with functionalist operationality or instrumental reason as the
basis of a free society.

Habermas traces the emergence of the public sphere and the actu-
alization of communicative rationality back to bourgeois efforts to
resist aristocratic hegemony. In his earliest work, *The Structural
Transformation of the Public Sphere* (1962), he traced the rise of a
public sphere in coffee houses, salons and lodges, relating it to the

spread of print culture in newspapers. In these social spaces a type of public speech was instituted which was characterized by (1) a disregard for status, (2) a putting into question of new areas of common concern, and (3) a principle of inclusivity, that is, that anyone who chose to could participate. Habermas sets as the basic condition for this public sphere the culture of the bourgeois household. In the newly constituted "privacy" of the family, a new subject emerged which was transferred to the "public sphere" of the coffee house. The bourgeois felt himself comfortable, at ease, human and morally affirmed in his home. In this setting a new subject was constituted that once in the coffee houses was autonomous, critical, free. "The communication of the public that debated critically about culture remained dependent on reading pursued in the closed-off privacy of the home."[10] In sum, Habermas thinks the culture of the white, male bourgeois instituted a form of communicative practice that if reinstituted in the late twentieth century provides the basis for universal freedom.

Habermas makes this argument despite the fact that the emancipatory politics of the 1970s and 1980s have concerned in good part an analysis of the limitations of bourgeois models, a critique of the position of the white, male subject and its pretensions to universality. Feminist, anti-racist and anti-colonial discourses have in many ways put into question the generalizability of the rational subject. They have shown how this universalization has worked against minority cultures, how it has served the interests of the established subject positions, how it makes Other all groups, races and sexes that do not conform to its image of autonomous individuality. Arjun Appadurai speaks directly to Habermas's attempt to universalize the bourgeois public sphere when he writes: "The master-narrative of the Enlightenment (and its many variants in England, France and the United States) was constructed with a certain internal logic and presupposed a certain relationship between reading, representation and the public sphere . . ."[11] What Habermas sees as the completion of the Enlightenment project of emancipation, Appadurai views as an extension of Western domination.

Appadurai argues that a new global culture is being set into place by dint of telecommunications technology and a general increase in worldwide intercourse. The incipient synergy of computers, telephone and television produces a cosmopolitan culture in which ethnic difference is evoked and registered. An enormous constellation of images, narratives and ideas is shared across the globe but indigenized by ethnicity and culture in very different ways. The key term "democracy" translates differently in different ideological and cultural landscapes. Neither universality nor homogeneity adequately expresses the emerging global culture. Rather a form of cosmopolitanism captures better the mixture of shared experience and difference without denying the enormous disparity of economic well-being that exists. Habermas, on the contrary, perceives in the new communications technologies only a corruption of communicative rationality:

> In comparison with printed communications the programs sent by the new media curtail the reactions of their recipients in a peculiar way. They draw the eyes and ears of the public under their spell but at the same time, by taking away its distance, place it under "tutelage," which is to say they deprive it of the opportunity to say something and to disagree. . . . The sounding board of an educated stratum tutored in the public use of reason has been shattered: the public is split apart into minorities of specialists who put their reason to use nonpublicly and the great mass of consumers whose receptiveness is public but uncritical. . . . The consensus developed in rational-critical public debate has yielded to compromise fought out or simply imposed nonpublicly. . . . Today conversation itself is administered.[12]

Going to the movies, listening to radio, watching TV, messaging by computer or FAX machine, using the telephone are all for Habermas only degradations of communicative rationality, examples of the colonization of the lifeworld by the system. One of the serious limitations of the theory of communicative rationality is that it cannot articulate language differences in electronically mediated communication, perceiving only the lack of what it calls "rationality."

But another interpretation is possible, one that derives from French poststructuralists, Habermas's opposition. As I have done in *The Mode of Information*, one can study the way subjects are constituted in these new electronically mediated language situations, looking precisely for configurations that call into question the privilege of the autonomous rational individual not to go behind it to some "rationalist" position but to test the possibility of emancipation in new subject positions, as Appadurai suggests. At this point aspects of the theoretical strategies of Lyotard, Baudrillard, Foucault, Derrida and Deleuze are most appropriate because they have initiated the project of examining the role of language in the constitution of subjectivity and they have done so with an effort to move outside the parameters and constraints of the Cartesian/Enlightenment position. From

Habermas's vantage point within those parameters it appears that poststructuralists advocate irrationality; but from the vantage point of poststructuralists, the position of rationality, with its particular relation to representation, reading and privacy (the ideal speech situation of the coffee house), is itself a stumbling block to the discovery of contemporary cultural processes that promote and reproduce domination.

The issue dividing Habermas and French poststructuralists is the relation of language to the subject in the era of electronically mediated communication. Habermas's position has the advantage of arguing for continuity with the Enlightenment liberal tradition, asking only for an extension of democracy to institute a public sphere for the enactment of communicative rationality, for a critique of incursions of the system into the lifeworld. French poststructuralists contend that Habermas's theory of communicative action, based on a "universal pragmatics" of validity claims, substitutes for the autonomous individual an interaction or practice of communicating subjects. Habermas, in their view, fails to reconceptualize the subject in relation to language, to articulate the way language constitutes the subject in different patterns. In their opinion, he reduces cultural or symbolic interaction to communicative action and further reduces this to the "rationality" of validity claims. Habermas's critique of instrumental rationality in favor of communicative rationality does get to the root of the problem of modernity, of the project of Enlightenment.

The subject for Habermas remains pre-given, pre-linguistic, and the movement of emancipation consists in removing structures of domination that have been placed on top of it.[13] Emancipation consists in a lifting of burdens, a releasing of potentials for freedom already contained by the subject. As transcendent, universal attributes of speech, communicative rationality requires no cultural change, no reconfiguration of the subject, no restructuring of language. The Habermasian critique of poststructuralist positions on the grounds that they do not distinguish between rationality and manipulation, between the legitimate influence of the better argument and sheer illocutionary force, does not convince.[14] The problem raised by Lyotard and others is not to find a defense of rationality but to enable cultural difference, what the Enlightenment theorized as "Other," to emerge against the performativity or rationality of the system. From the poststructuralist perspective, the telos of consensus that Habermas evokes is itself a form of domination since the authority of the better argument to which all participants must submit necessarily erases the difference of subject positions and stabilizes or essentializes one subject position in particular. And it is thus a form of coercion.

The effort of poststructuralists has been to articulate the mechanisms through which language is more than constative, representational, univocal, the ways in which word and thing do not gel into an eternal stability. This critique has uncovered the figure of the subject that stood behind such stability and the dualist metaphysic of subject as agent/object as passive material that provided its foundation. The theory of writing in Derrida, of the imaginary in Lacan, of discourse/ practice in Foucault, of the differend in Lyotard, of the hyper-real in Baudrillard are all aimed at subverting the paradigm of the subject and its relation to language which has dominated Western culture at least since Descartes and the Enlightenment. Whatever epistemological force one may accord to the work of the poststructuralists, one must acknowledge the fruitfulness of their position in relation to the politics of feminism and anti-colonial discourse as well as to the emergence of the mode of information. In both cases a convergence exists between the poststructuralist effort to reconstruct the figure of the rational subject with the inscription of non-instrumental, destabilized subjects in electronically mediated communication, on the one hand, and critique of white male culture from positions outside of it on the other hand.[15]

Thus far, however, it must be acknowledged that the French critique of the subject has not led to a new politics. Habermasian critics, not surprised by this deficiency, complain that poststructuralists have no political agenda, maintain no clear norms to guide practice, and have no general perspective on social development and no vision of a better future.[16] While these complaints must largely be sustained, poststructuralists reply that they are precisely the issues that must be expunged from the discourse of intellectuals. The "normal" expectations of such discourse from the Enlightenment to the 1960s were that it provide a coherent sense of the social world, distinguish salient historical trends, specify groups suffering structural domination and therefore having potentials to mobilize for change, and finally depict utopian possibilities.[17] Habermas's theory of communicative rationality accomplishes all of these tasks whereas the French poststructuralists achieve probably none of them.

The French thinkers, in particular Foucault, Derrida and Lyotard, strive to rid their discourse of concepts that present a closed or sutured understanding of society by which they refer to theories that totalize from one level, reduce multiplicity into unity, or organize discourse toward an end or telos which is usually utopian. Any concepts that fix identities, stabilize meanings or resolve the nature of society are improper and politically dangerous, contend the poststructuralists.[18] Because of these self-imposed restrictions, French poststructuralist theory fails to satisfy certain assumptions about completion. The reader is often bothered by missing elements or gaps in the discourse that Habermasian writing furnishes. Some readers go so far as to complain that French poststructuralism can say nothing "positive" about "reality," that it is "narcissistic" or, worse, "nihilist." The French writers reply that they do not want to reproduce at the level of theory the pattern of reason as control that is found both in society and in the tradition of critical social theory. Critical theory in the past, they argue, was able to define the radical moment of society and ground progressive politics only by constituting a suspect theoretical subject. This subject was a stable point of knowledge set against a passive world of objects over which it was to establish a position of control through its discourse. In this sense criticism must avoid the metaphysical gesture of grounding itself in the absolute even at the cost of failing to satisfy "logical" demands for coherence and closure.[19]

Lyotard exemplifies the poststructuralist reluctance to closure. In *The Postmodern Condition* he warns that the trend toward computerization implies the reduction of language to the level of "performativity" or efficiency. The theoretical concept in this case represents the real as a closed system governed by instrumentality. Society is seen as a unified system of information flows in which the goal of theory is to insure the maximum ratio of sense over noise. For Lyotard, theory here becomes a "terrorist" denial of difference. In response he urges critical theory to move to a notion of the unrepresentable, to that which cannot be captured by concept, that which resists the logic of performativity and which therefore serves as a basis for an idea of justice based on the acceptance of an agon of multiple discourses or differends. Theory retreats to locate the minimal conditions for justice, withdraws to the defense of the little narrative against all positions that assert grand gestures or metanarratives, all projects of Enlightenment which solve "the riddle history" or dialectically realize the absolute spirit. The sense one gets from reading Lyotard is that, to quote Hebdige quoting the Talking Heads, we are on the road to nowhere, not on the grand boulevard of progress.[20]

Poststructuralism's apparent retreat to a minimalist position might be interpreted as the pessimism of white male theory in an age of decolonization (the decentering of Europe) and feminism. The easy assumption of the voice of the universal that has been a hallmark of white male Western theorizing no longer rings true. Attention must now be paid to the gender and ethnicity of the thinker not because of some simple, unilinear determinism of these factors but because the positionality of the theorizing subject inevitably bears traces of sex and race. In addition we learn from the history of the comfortable appropriation of the universal by white Western males that any such appropriation gives cause for concern. When one accepts as an inevitable condition that theoretical subjects are fully gendered and ethnically specific, a new form of dialogue might begin in a context of what I would call differentiated cosmopolitanism, not the flat homogeneity of earlier claims to universality as exemplified by Habermas.

Differentiated cosmopolitanism is furthered by the thickening and intensification of communication across boundaries of locality, a process enabled but not completely shaped by electronic forms of communication. Previously subjugated voices are more readily brought to one's attention and previously private speech and practice of elites are available for all to see. President Bush's regurgitation at a Japanese state dinner illustrates the latter, and the well-known photograph of the Vietnamese girl running on a road with body contorted by pain illustrates the former. Elite control over information slips from its grasp as info-bites from dominated groups bleep through communication channels. While the global communication village is not at all a democracy, enough local knowledges do make their appearance to shatter the uncontested hegemony of male Western culture. I believe this structural feature of the present warrants the periodization "postmodernity."

And yet such postmodern cosmopolitanism urges the poststructuralist further toward a minimal theoretical posture. For another bastion of modernist social theory is the assumption that a community of face-to-face individuals is definable, however different its form may take in the varieties of Enlightenment traditions. Postmodernist minimalism, then, might equally be interpreted as a response to the collapse of any hope for a free community in an age of electronically mediated communication. One may argue that critical social theory, from its beginning through the recent work of Habermas, has assumed as the goal or at least as a possibility of history a democratic social order in which face-to-face relations between individuals transpire with a minimum mediation of structures of domination, hierarchy or asymmetry. But the dramatic spread of electronic communication systems which will undoubtedly rise even more precipitously once the computer, the telephone and the television are systematically integrated toll the end of community in any shape it has hitherto been imagined. The mode of information betokens a restructuring of language so drastic that the figure of the subject that it will constitute cannot readily be discerned. Relations of mind to body, person to person, humanity to nature are undergoing such profound reconfiguration that images of community are presented if at all only in science fiction books and films. Poststructuralist theory, I contend, reflects these changes by redefining critical discourse to bypass reliance on either the autonomous rational individual or the democratic face-to-face community.

French poststructuralism has the advantage over Habermasian critical theory in facing squarely the question of the postmodern, of the prospects of critique in an age that no longer enjoys the supports, metaphysical and social, of the modern Enlightenment era. The issue of the postmodern evokes a consistent negative response from Habermas in *The Philosophical Discourse of Modernity*, where he attacks Derrida and Foucault as postmodern irrationalists. Among the French theorists only Lyotard has consistently employed the category of the postmodern, and even then only ambivalently. Nonetheless French poststructuralists, I argue, defend the modern/postmodern distinction in the sense that their critique begins by putting into question the validity of modern positions. Because they confront squarely the dilemma of the subject in the postmodern age they are surer guides to a reconstruction of critical social theory than Habermas. In the present-day context of German unification, East European and Russian social and political reorganization and general European centralization, French poststructuralists may appear deficient for speaking very little on urgent affairs. Yet as these issues become sorted out, Europe will surely face the problem of the postmodern and the work of the poststructuralists will likely become an important resort in the discussions.

The issue of the postmodern addresses political topics at a very general level. Recent poststructuralist works such as Lyotard's *The Inhuman*[21] and Haraway's *Simians, Cyborgs and Women*[22] register the depths of postmodern culture in a recognition of an emerging "inhuman" or transhuman social order. The referential anchor of the individual recedes in social prominence as global communication networks (Lyotard) and human/machine combinations (Haraway) replace older figures of man versus nature and individual versus society. If we are witnessing a general reconfiguration of the most fundamental features of the socio-cultural, some care must be taken in connecting the theme of the postmodern to particular or local political issues. When focusing on the politics of postmodernity there is a danger that the general processes at stake will become confused with or reduced to the politics of modernity. For example, the controversy over multiculturalism, which is often identified as a postmodern issue, easily slides into the terms and references of liberal politics, of pluralism and even of the American consensus politics of "the melting pot." I shall discuss the relation of multiculturalism to postmodern politics bearing in mind the above considerations.

The term multiculturalism generally refers to curricular reform at institutions of higher learning. As more and more minorities attend these institutions, the easy assumption of the universality of Western culture, the Eurocentrism of many basic courses in the humanities and social sciences, increasingly appears incongruous. On campus after campus, controversial curricular reforms have been initiated by faculty and more often by administrators to include non-Western or minority components in courses on literature and history. For conservatives such as Lynn Chaney, multiculturalist reforms signal a deep threat to the quality of higher education, since it happens that, for her, excellence and white are indissociable attributes. Some liberals attempt to assimilate multiculturalism to consensus politics: here racial and ethnic minorities in the present context are equated with European immigrants of earlier decades and are to be treated similarly. Curricular reform for this group means devoting study to African-Americans, for example, along with Italian, Jewish and Irish immigrants. In both cases, liberals retain the notion of pluralist consensus by which all communities are welcome to melt down their identities in the crucible of modern democracy, capitalism and urbanism.

A third position associates multiculturalism with postmodernism, and it is to this position that I want to address my remarks because it opens the question of politics in relation to postmodernism. The argument in this case is that the inclusion of non-European cultures in the curriculum introduces a multiplicity of viewpoints that corresponds to the postmodernist celebration of difference. An essay by Tom Bridges, for example, argues that "anyone wishing to pursue the reform of the curriculum along multiculturalist lines simply cannot avoid confronting and dealing with the issues raised by postmodernism."[23] Postmodernism and multiculturalism share a rejection of the universalist claims of the Enlightenment, he contends, making them interdependent and politically similar. Lyotard's appeal for the small story over the grand narrative and Foucault's call for an "insurrection of subjugated knowledges" fit into this profile. In such a spirit, Foucault wants "to entertain the claims to attention of local, discontinuous, disqualified, illegitimate knowledges against the claims of a unitary body of theory which would filter, hierarchise and order them in the name of some true knowledge and some arbitrary idea of what constitutes a science and its objects."[24] The suspicion of the Enlightenment posture of universal rationality appears to emerge with equal, parallel ferocity among postmodernists and multiculturalists.

But this alliance is a troubled one and it is troubled in ways that reveal the limitations of both positions to extract themselves from Enlightenment positions and politics. In the case of the postmodernists, the difficulty concerns their repetition in denial of the Enlightenment *posture* of critique, their replication of Enlightenment *forms* of critique (the writing of discourses) and their address of universalist themes (society *at large* for Lyotard consists of differends) while at the same time denying universalist claims. In its rules of formation, then, the discourse of postmodernism retains these crucial Enlightenment characteristics. While postmodernists attempt to avoid foundationalism, the systematic elaboration of theory out of an ontologically secure subject position, they have not completely altered the discursive form of modernity, nor its institutional apparatuses.

In the case of the multiculturalists, the difficulty concerns a reliance on subject positions that reproduce Enlightenment notions of agency. Minority discourse may function critically as an other to Enlightenment subject positions, but the assertion of validity for minority positions often reproduces the fullness of identity that is a major problem in the Enlightenment position itself. In a recent collection of essays representing a broad array of many of the best writers on the question of cultural difference, the issue of identity, agency and subject position appears over and over again as the bane of critical thinking.[25] The colossal problem is one of asserting the emancipatory potential of multiculturalist subject positions while avoiding the essentialism or self-identity that is associated with Enlightenment forms of resistance. Over and over writers on this subject reiterate the warning that the position of the other is neither a guarantee of ethico-political superiority nor a fixed, coherent wholeness. The critical potential of the "other" position must be carefully extracted from the structure of its domination.

With postmodern discourses such as those of Lyotard and Foucault it is often noted that non-Western minorities function as an empty alterity, providing a standpoint of critique of Western logocentrism, but one vacant of specificity.[26] Yet when that position of alterity is "filled in" or "completed" by multiculturalists, the resulting subject position often becomes a self-identical one and its culture uncritically affirmed. For example, when some Asian-American students are asked in class to present a critique of the writer under discussion, they refuse and justify that refusal by referring to their local culture's or family's prohibition of criticism. It does not matter to them that the writer in question might be a racist or an anti-multiculturalist. The fact that the writer is read in the context of an institution of higher learning is enough to forestall criticism. In this case the resort to the legitimacy of the minority culture prevents the critique of positions that would refuse that culture's presence in the curriculum. This example is by no means unique and the same problem is found in any number of "other" positions. In other words the postmodernist validation of minority discourse as a consequence of the critique of Enlightenment universalism, when set into the academic multiculturalist arena, may allow no doubts to be raised about the specificity of ethnic and racial discourse even when the text in question denies the critical function of education in favor of instrumental ones. If a multiculturalist curriculum would decenter learning from Enlightenment universalism and include the experience of non-Western groups, postmodernist configurations of critique may well be incapable of providing an adequate framework for that study.

This political limitation of postmodernist thought, however, ought not surprise anyone. In my view postmodernism is a fledgling position, one registering changes in society (the demise of colonialism, the spread of electronically mediated communication, etc.) that have only begun to revolutionize the structures of modernity. Postmodernism anticipates a future in which these tendencies will no longer be emergent but dominant. In the meantime the major modern political tendencies, shorn to be sure of their legitimating metanarratives, continue to plod along, blanketing the play of forces with discursive regimes that hold back or disguise as much as they can postmodern developments. In this complex, ambiguous situation multiculturalists must choose between a Habermasian universalism that denies their enunciative position altogether and postmodernist differentialism that affirms that position but cannot fully defend that affirmation.

4

The Mode of Information and Postmodernity

A poststructuralist approach to communication theory analyzes the way electronically mediated communication (what I call "the mode of information") both challenges and reinforces systems of domination that are emerging in a postmodern society and culture.[1] My general thesis is that the mode of information enacts a radical reconfiguration of language, one which constitutes subjects outside the pattern of the rational, autonomous individual. This familiar modern subject is displaced by the mode of information in favor of one that is multiplied, disseminated and decentered, continuously interpellated as an unstable identity. At the level of culture, this instability poses both dangers and challenges which, if they become part of a political movement, or are connected with the politics of feminism, ethnic/racial minorities, gay and lesbian positions, may lead to a fundamental challenge to modern social institutions and structures.

Communication theory needs to account for electronically mediated communication and by doing so take its proper place of importance in general social theory. This importance has not generally been recognized by the great theorists of modern society who emphasized action (labor) and institutions (bureaucracy) over language and communication. Marx and Weber, for example, fall clearly within this tendency. Yet their theories reflect the dominant communicational mode of their time, even though they failed fully to take it into account. They were heirs of the eighteenth-century Enlightenment, an intellectual tradition that was profoundly rooted in print culture. The Enlightenment theory of the autonomous rational individual derived much sustenance and reinforcement from the practice of reading the printed page.[2] Hegel struck such a chord when he referred to newspaper reading as "the morning prayer of modern man." The spatial materiality of print – the linear display of sentences, the stability of the word on the page, the orderly, systematic spacing of black letters on a white background – enables readers to distance themselves from authors. These features of print promote an ideology of the critical individual, reading and thinking in isolation, outside the network of political and religious dependencies. In an opposite but yet complementary way print culture, by the materiality of the word on the page as compared with the evanescence of the word in oral culture, promotes the authority of the author, the intellectual and the theorist. This double movement engenders the reader as critic and the author as authority, an apparent opposition or contradiction but actually an oscillation of dominance characteristic of communication in modern society.

In the case of both the reader and the author, print culture constitutes the individual as a subject, as transcendent to objects, as stable and fixed in identity, in short, as a grounded essence. And this feature of print culture is homologous with the figure of the subject in modern institutions – the capitalist market with its possessive individuals, the legal system with its "reasonable man," representative democracy with its secret ballots and presumption of individual self-interest, bureaucracy with its instrumental rationality, the factory with its Taylorite system, the educational system with its individualized examinations and records. In response to these developments, Marx theorized the emancipation of rational individuality through the class struggle and Weber regretted the fixing of instrumental rationality in unchangeable social organizations. Both presumed a configuration of the subject which was a product of print culture and both viewed modernity as the final instantiation of that social individual. However, both missed the role of communications in the process of constituting such subjects and both understood the process of subject constitution only in part. Marx realized that individuals change in different modes of production, but posited man as a "species being" that communism would fully actualize, one that looks very much like the Enlightenment's autonomous rational agent. Weber allowed four types of subject (value rational, instrumental rational, emotional and traditional) and understood them as in some sense historically produced, but saw modernity as inscribing only one, the instrumental rational. For both men history ended with the appearance of the autonomous rational agent as subject, as fixed essence.

The emergence of the mode of information, with its electronically mediated systems of communication, changes the way we think about the subject and promises to alter as well the shape of society. Electronic culture promotes the individual as an unstable identity, as a continuous process of multiple identity formation, and raises the question of a social form beyond the modern, the possibility of a postmodern society.[3] Electronic culture promotes theories (such as poststructuralism) that focus on the role of language in the process of the constitution of subjects and that undermine views of the reader and author as stable points of criticism and authority respectively. When print mediates the theorist's understanding of the subject, language is understood as representational, as an arbitrary system of signs, invoked by a thinker in order to point to objects. As long as this regime is in place, the subject remains a stable point, fixed in space and time. Figures that upset such an understanding of the subject – women, children, non-Europeans – are placed in the position of being Other, of not being taken seriously into account. When electronic communications are a factor in the theorist's understanding of the subject, language is understood as performative, rhetorical, as an active figuring and positioning of the subject. With the spread of this regime of communications, the subject can only be understood as partially stable, as repeatedly reconfigured at different points of time and space, as non-self-identical and therefore as always partly Other.

Electronic communications, like print, place a distance between the addressor and the addressee; they accentuate the feature of language that permits a gap between the speaker and the listener. This gap is often understood by proponents of modern print-oriented theory as efficiency. From smoke signals to communication satellites, the principle is the same: extend the human voice. Just as tools may heighten the powers of the muscles in the production of goods, they may amplify the larynx, allowing speech at a distance. Theories that view communications technology purely as a question of efficiency unduly discourage new questions that arise from electronic communications, placing them within the older paradigms generated to theorize oral and print culture. When electronic communications are seen as simply allowing greater spatial and temporal extension, the analyst reconfirms the figure of the autonomous rational individual and reinstates the stability of the subject.

In terms of politics, oral communications, from the point of view of print culture, bind the individual in relations of political domination. When communications are restricted to speech (and manuscript as its simple extension), individuals are easily restrained in ties of dependence. By enlarging the gap mentioned above as inherent in language, print allows a distance to intervene between speaker and listener and this gap permits the individual to think, coolly to judge the words of the other without his or her overbearing presence. Or so advocates of print culture contend.

Theorists of print culture interpret the gap as enhancing the powers of reason, enabling individual autonomy. Proponents of print culture, in other words, link the gap in language to the subject as centered in reason. The ideological force of modern Enlightenment communication theory derives in good part from this move, a move that incorporates print technology within modern social theory. But the stability of this move is always partial, always threatened. For the gap instantiated by print could be turned against modern theory: it could be appropriated by excluded groups such as workers, women and non-Europeans to promote their ends; it could be turned into cultural resistance as in avant-garde art movements since the romantic period.[4] Nineteenth-century jeremiads against the dangers of reading novels are indications that the inducement to fantasy was one appropriation of the gap that resisted its Enlightenment containment. As early as Rousseau's *Emile*, Sophie falls in love with Emile because he resembles a character in a novel she read. Love was mediated by the gap inscribed in print.

Electronic culture permits a different interpretation of the gap. The tremendous extension of the space between speaker and listener in the mode of information upsets the confinement of the gap to the self-identical subject. The combination of enormous distances with temporal immediacy produced by electronic communications both removes the speaker from the listener and brings them together. These opposing tendencies – opposite from the point of view of print culture – reconfigures the position of the individual so drastically that the figure of the self, fixed in time and space, capable of exercising cognitive control over surrounding objects, may no longer be sustained. Language no longer represents a reality, no longer is a neutral tool to enhance the subject's instrumental rationality: language becomes or better reconfigures reality. And by doing so the subject is interpellated through language and cannot easily escape recognition of that interpellation. Electronic communications systematically remove the fixed points, the grounds, the foundations that were essential to modern theory. I shall illustrate these transformations of cultural and social life by diverse examples of electronically mediated communication: the TV ad, the database and computer writing. And I shall explore these examples from the poststructuralist perspectives of Jean Baudrillard, Michel Foucault and Jacques Derrida.

In the register of humanist morality, TV ads are manipulative, deceptive and repugnant; they entice consumer decisions on "irrational" grounds and encourage a "quick fix" drug mentality as a false solution to life's problems. In the register of marketing, TV ads are evaluated in relation to their ability "to create effective demand" for the product. In the register of democratic politics, TV ads undermine the independent thinking of the electorate, diminishing its ability to distinguish truth from falsity, the real and the imaginary, and passify it into a state of indifference. In the register of Marxist social criticism, TV ads stimulate false needs that detract from the revolutionary purpose of the working class and serve only to pump up an economy that is beyond the control of the producers. Each of these perspectives contains a degree of validity but none approaches the crucial issue of the role of TV ads in contemporary culture, none reveals the altered language structure of the ads, and, most importantly, none draws attention to the relation of language to culture in the constitution of new subject positions, that is, new places in the network of social communication. I contend that TV ads exploit electronic mediation so as to inscribe a new technology of power, one whose political effects need to be assessed in relation to the possible emergence of a postmodern society.

Like monologues, print and radio, TV ads are nominally unidirectional communications: the sender addresses the receiver. Yet all communications enable responses, feedbacks, replies, however delayed. Monologues are subject to interventions, print to reposts or to conversations, radio to telephone call-ins. But each of these communication technologies is enunciated as unidirectional. The TV ad, unlike the other examples, easily combines images and sounds and writing. It displays moving, aural narratives of everyday reality at times with great verisimilitude. Because they control the context, the background, as well as the text of the narrative, TV ads contain special powers. The "reality" they represent can be "hyper-real," editing in contents not normally found together in "reality." Voice-overs, as another example, inject a super-ego-like authority in the ad. With great flexibility the ad constructs a mini-reality in which things are set in juxtapositions that violate the rules of the everyday. In particular, TV ads associate meanings, connotations and moods that are inappropriate in reality, subject to objections in dialogic communications, but effective at the level of desire, the unconscious, the imaginary. TV ads constitute a language system that leaves out the referent, the symbolic and the real, working instead with chains of signifiers (words) and signifieds (mental images). The referent, the symbolic and the real are absent and come into play only if the viewer buys the product.

The meaning structure of the TV ad, strictly keeping itself to the levels of signifiers, meanings and images, powerfully invites the viewer to identify with the commodity. The ad stimulates not an object choice, a cognitive decision, a rational evaluation, but works at other linguistic levels to produce the effects of incorporation and attachment between the viewer and the product. The viewer is the absent hero or heroine of the ad. The viewer is solicited to displace him or herself into the ad and become one with the meanings associated with the product. In its monologue, in its construction of context and its association of non-connected meanings, the TV ad inscribes a new pattern of communication into the culture, one repeated ad infinitum, one extended, I need hardly remind you, to politics, religion and every conceivable aspect of social life.

Through these communications, the realist linguistic paradigm is shaken. The TV ad works with simulacra, with inventions and with imaginings. The modernist print-oriented communications associated with education, capitalism/socialism, bureaucracy and representative democracy – identities centered in Weber's instrumental reason – are displaced in favor of a postmodernist, electronic-oriented communication in which identity is destabilized and fragmented. This is accomplished not in the highly ritualized collective action of religion or other community function, but in the privacy, informality and isolation of the home. And it is accomplished not at special moments of the calendar, but every day and for long hours. The population places itself in communication situations in which the TV ad is the norm of language construction, and the effects on the construction of subject positions are no doubt profound.

Jean Baudrillard, in *Consumer Society, The System of Objects* and *For a Critique of the Political Economy of the Sign*, began the line of thinking about contemporary culture which I am pursuing in relation to TV ads as part of the mode of information.[5] Baudrillard broke with the realist paradigms of social science at first by combining Roland Barthes' semiology with the neo-Marxism of Henri Lefebvre. In the late 1960s and early 1970s, he attempted to move social critique from the level of action to that of language. He began to look at consumer culture not as a process of Veblenesque mimesis, of "keeping up with the Joneses," of conformist behavior, but as a peculiar restructuring of signs. Structuralist linguists had shown that meaning was a result of relations of difference between words. The key to language was not so much a connection between a word and a thing but an arbitrary designation that depended on a differential mark. Language for them was composed of binary oppositions of signifiers – I/you, black/white, and so forth – whose ability to have meaning hinged on the stable relation between the terms or what they termed the "structure." Language was theorized as a vast machine for generating such differential relations. But in order to grasp this the theorist needed to shift his or her point of view away from the individual as a subject who produced and received meaning to language as an objective system of relations. In other words, language became intelligible only from the standpoint of its structure; language then constituted the subject, not the reverse.

For Baudrillard the structuralists are too formalist, restricting themselves too closely to linguistic signs. He shifts the object of analysis to daily life, taking society itself as the field for interpretation. Consumer activity would then be seen as a circulation of signs in the structuralist sense. The commodity is thus extracted from the domain of economic theory or moral commentary and viewed as a complex code. The key to consumerism is not an irrational tendency to conspicuous display but the insertion of individuals into a communications relation in which they receive messages in the form of commodities. The consumer is not "irrational" and the object is not a "utility." Between the poles of object and intention is the advertisement which disrupts the normal set of differential relations of signs. The ad presupposes language not as a reference to a "real" but as an arbitrary connection of signifiers. It simply rearranges those signifiers, violating their "normal" references. The aim of the ad is to associate a chain of signifiers in a narrative of a desirable life style: Pepsi = youth = sexiness = popularity = fun, for example.

The status of the ad as a linguistic and cultural phenomenon, Baudrillard argued in the 1980s, is that of a simulacrum, a copy that has no original, has no objective referent. For him today's culture increasingly is composed of these simulacra which taken together compose a new order of reality, which he terms "the hyper-real." Culture consists of constructed realities, Disneylands, which are more real than the real they are supposed to refer back to. But in the end there is no reference back since, once social life is presented as a theme park in one place, its constructed element emerges and tends to dominate over its presence as a fixed, natural order. Society becomes a collage of theme parks which one enters at will (and for a price). Baudrillard totalizes his view of the hyper-real, dismissing other modernist perspectives on politics and the economy as without value. By contextualizing his understanding of consumer culture in relation to the mode of information, by connecting it with specific communication technologies, I hope to extract the critical impulse of his position without acceding to his monolithic vision.

Computerized databases are another form of electronically mediated communication that have been studied from various perspectives. Liberal writers have rightly been concerned that the vast data accumulated in this form and its relative ease of transfer pose a threat to the privacy of the individual. With so much information about individuals now digitalized in databases, one's life becomes an open book for those who have access to the right computers. Agencies of all kinds – military, police, governmental, corporate – continuously gather data and exchange it from one computer to another while the individuals to whom this data refers have little control over its flow or, in many cases, knowledge of its existence. In the eyes of liberals, society is indeed nearing the nightmare of 1984, only a few years behind Orwell's schedule. Marxists for their part have shown how databases are a new form of information as commodity, one which has passed largely into the control of the biggest corporations. Increasingly society becomes divided into the information rich and the information poor. Existing class divisions on a national and even a global scale are reinforced and further sedimented by the technology of computerized information. As the economy relies more and more upon information, access to databases is not at all a trivial matter. The fate of companies, even nations, hinges upon the timely procurement of information. In comparison with feudal regimes, capitalist societies once prided themselves on establishing the free flow of information, thinking of this feature of modernity as a touchstone of freedom. The digitalization of information in the form of databases acts to facilitate its instantaneous, global availability, so the restraint of commodification flies in the face of the advance of the technology.

While these perspectives are valuable for a full understanding of the database as a communications technology, they neglect a fundamental aspect of the phenomenon: its ability to constitute and multiply the identity of the individual and thereby to promote his/her control. The social model implicit in the above positions is one of individuals/groups confronting institutions and social forces in a relation of struggle, contest and opposition. At the most general level, liberals and Marxists assume a world of discrete, stable entities. Hence the notion of privacy, for example, with its sense of a microworld in which individuals are sequestered from others and about which no one has knowledge without the explicit agreement of those individuals. Without such privacy, liberals contend, resistance to the state is impossible because privacy is a sort of small cloud within which critical reason may safely function, the space of independent thought, distant from the influence of the phenomenal, perceptual world of the senses. Liberals value urbanism precisely for its tendency to lose the individual in the anonymity of the crowd, in contrast with the rural village in which everyone knows everything about everyone else. The city, for them, is the locus of freedom, paradoxically because its density of population is an obscuring mask behind which the atomized individual may secure independent thought.

The contemporary urban quotidian strips the mask away. Individual actions now leave trails of digitized information which are regularly accumulated in computer databases and, at the speed of light or sound, transmitted back and forth between computers. Previously anonymous actions such as paying for a dinner, borrowing a book from a library, renting a videotape from a rental store, subscribing to a magazine, making a long distance telephone call – all by interacting with perfect strangers – now are wrapped in a clothing of information traces which are gathered and arranged into profiles, forming more and more detailed portraits of individuals. This postmodern daily life is not one of discrete individuals, hidden behind shields of anonymity in market interactions with strangers; nor is it a return to a village of familiar faces.[6] Instead it combines features of both without the advantages of either. In the credit card payment for dinner, the waiter is a stranger but the computer which receives the information "knows" the customer very well. Urban life now consists of face-to-face interactions with strangers coupled by electronically mediated interactions with machines "familiar" with us. The lines dividing individual from individual and individual from institution are consistently crossed by computer databases, cancelling privacy as a model of action or even as an issue.

Information flows today double the action of individuals and subvert theoretical models which presuppose either privacy or the class struggle. Society is now a double movement: one, of individuals and institutions; another, of information flows. A recent television drama, for example, depicted the fine-grained level of current information retrieval. A murderer attempted to secure his alibi by leaving a message on the answering machine of the person he murdered, falsifying the time of the call. But he did so from his cellular car phone so that the police were able to find out the actual time of the call, because all such calls are logged by the cellular phone company. The murderer took into account one aspect of the mode of information (answering machines) but forgot another, the traces left in databases by calls from car phones.

Databases are inherently limited and restricted structures of information. Unlike the narratives, which are complex and flexible, they are severely restricted forms of discourse. In database programs only certain marks may be made in certain "fields" or areas. For instance, if, after the name of the individual, a "field" for magazine subscriptions follows, normally one cannot fill this field with the name of the magazine, but only with a code for certain groups of magazines. Thus *The New Republic* might be coded as "l" for liberal and *The Guardian* as "r" for radical. If video rentals are included in the database, *Deep Throat* and *Last Tango in Paris* might both be coded as "x." Such simplification of data drastically distorts, one might complain, particular experience, but it also vastly facilitates the speed with which information may be retrieved. In this way, databases configure reality, make composites of individual experience, that could be characterized as caricatures. By contrast, databases may also include graphics, that is to say, pictures or copies of fingerprints, for example. Information about individuals then becomes much more complex. The important consideration, however, is not the question of verisimilitude: would any individual be pleased by the accuracy of the information portrait contained in a database? But rather that databases constitute additional identities for individuals, identities which – in the interactions between computers and between institutions which rely upon them, on the one hand, and individuals on the other – take the place of those individuals. When a computer search is done for John Smith, the output from the machine is, from the point of view of the receiving computer or institution, John Smith himself. Just as actions in daily life are doubled by information traces, so identities are multiplied in the interactions of computer databases.

The theoretical problem of accounting for the social impact of databases is best assisted by the work of Michel Foucault. This is so in three senses: Foucault theorized, first, power in relation to a specific social formation, the panopticon, which has direct application to databases; second, the relation between social phenomena and the subject that is relevant to the case of databases; and third, the relation between discourse and practice, ideas and action, attitudes and behavior in a way that permits the understanding of databases outside the limitations of the paradigms of liberal and Marxist theory.

In *Discipline and Punish* Foucault uses the term "panopticon" to designate the control mechanism in prisons by which a guard, stationed in a central tower, could observe the inmates, arranged in cells around the tower with windows facing in toward the tower, without himself being seen by them.[7] Panopticon, literally "all-seeing," denotes a form of power which attempts to orient the prisoners toward the authority system of the prison as a step in their reformation or normalization. For the process of reform, the panopticon is a part of a broader set of mechanisms which included a minutely regulated schedule, a file-keeping system on each prisoner, and so forth. What interests Foucault in the system of discipline is not only its micrological detail but also its "positive" inscription of power. Unlike the central government which uses power as a "negative" principle of preventing or denying certain activities, the panopticon shapes and molds the behavior of the criminals, producing, in a sense, a new person, the prison inmate. The key to the mechanism of discipline is the continuous, systematic, unobserved surveillance of a population. The criminal is coerced to follow a plan and to be aware that the slightest deviation on his part from the plan would be observed and would have consequences for him. Through the workings of the panopticon, a norm is imposed on a population, on its practices and its attitudes, a norm that is a result not of the imposition of someone else's will, as in feudalism, but rather of an anonymous authority that is seemingly omnipresent. In the panopticon Foucault locates a system of power at the level of the everyday, as opposed to the level of the state, which combines discourses and practices to instantiate the social character of the inmate. As a general feature of society, the panopticon is an example of what Foucault calls a "technology of power" or a "microphysics of power."

In a second way Foucault's theory of the panopticon applies to databases. As a positive instantiation of power, the panopticon constitutes the individual criminal as an inmate. The discourse/practice of discipline produces the behaviors and attitudes of the prison population, regardless of the degree to which the prisoners resist or subvert that imposition. Their identity becomes that of an inmate however enthusiastic they may or may not have been about such a fate. By the same token, databases in the super-panopticon constitute identities for each individual and they do so regardless of whether the individual is even aware of it. Individuals are "known" to computer databases, have distinct "personalities" for them and in relation to which the computer "treats" them in programmed ways. These identities also serve as a basis for the communication between computers, communications that occur routinely and without the knowledge of the "real person." Such identities are hardly innocent since they may seriously affect the individual's life, serving as the basis for a denial of credit, or an FBI investigation, or the termination of social assistance, or the denial of employment or residence. In each case the individual is acted upon in relation to his or her identity as it is constituted in the database. Simply because this identity has no intimate connection with the internal consciousness of the individual, with his or her self-defined attributes, in no way minimizes its force or effectiveness. With the dissemination of databases, a communications technology pervades the social space and multiplies the identity of individuals, regardless of their will, intention, feeling or cognition.

In order fully to comprehend the significance of the constitution of identities by databases, one must appreciate the epistemological break Foucault enacts with the commonplace sense of the distinction between action and language, behavior and intention, a distinction that is one of the hallmarks of modern social theory. In relation to the social import of databases, Marxists, for example, concern themselves with the use made of databases by the state and the corporations. They criticize the way these organizations use databases to enhance their control and power over subordinate classes. In their work they maintain a clear distinction between institutions and individuals, action and knowledge, behavior and information. The state is a force external to individuals, an institution whose power increases by dint of the tool of databases. The vast information at the state's disposal constitutes another link in the chain of oppression. By contrast Foucault focuses on the way power is both action and knowledge and the way power implicates the individual. He looks for the connections between phenomena which others see as discrete oppositions. The science of criminology for him is simply another element in the mechanism of discipline, not a privileged locus of truth outside the play of power. Similarly the individual's identity is not outside power but constituted by its operations, linked to it inextricably. The super-panopticon then emerges not as an imposition or restraint upon the individual but rather as part of the individual's identity. Foucault's ability to specify the relation panopticon–inmate derives from his poststructuralist rejection of the separation of mind and body, language and action, ideology and institution in favor of their mutual imbrication. My analysis of databases, following Foucault, moves to a model of communication in which the level of the subject is not cut off from practice, the body, power, institutions.

Databases, I argue, operate as a super-panopticon. Like the prison, databases work continuously, systematically and surreptitiously, accumulating information about individuals and composing it into profiles. Unlike the panopticon, the "inmates" need not be housed in any architecture; they need only proceed with their regular daily life. The super-panopticon is thereby more unobtrusive than its forebear, yet it is no less efficient at its task of normalization. Each characteristic of an individual's profile in a database is easily distinguished for unusual qualities, from credit ratings and overdue book notices to excessive traffic violations. Another advantage of the newer power mechanism over the older one is its facility of communications, or transport of information. Computers easily exchange databases, the information in one being accessible to others. Instantaneously, across the globe information from databases flows in cyberspace to keep tabs on people. Databases "survey" us without the eyes of any prison guard and they do so more accurately and thoroughly than any human being. A major impact of the super-panopticon is that the distinction between public and private loses its force since it depended on an individual's space of invisibility, of opaqueness to the state and the corporations. Yet these characteristics are cancelled by databases because wherever one is and whatever one is doing, traces are left behind, traces that are transformed into information for the grist of computers.

Electronic writing is the third example of the mode of information as a communications technology. It covers a wide variety of writing practices, including word processing[8] and hypertext,[9] electronic mail and message services and computer conferencing. In each case the computer mediates the relation of author and reader, altering the basic conditions of the enunciation and reception of meaning.[10] Electronic writing continues the tendency begun with handwriting and print: it enables the removal of the author from the text, increases the distance, both spatial and temporal, of the author from the reader and augments the problem of the interpretation of texts. Compared with speech, writing is a way of storing language, fixing it so that it can be read by those not directly intended by the author. Writing thus promotes the transmission of culture from generation to generation, the transformation of cultural works into monuments and the elevation of authors into authorities. Writing also fosters the development of critical thinking on the part of the reader: by stabilizing words on the page, the reader can reflect upon them, go back to earlier passages and re-examine links of argument, and accomplish all of this in isolation without the presence of the author or the community exerting any pressure on the act of interpretation. Printing is often credited with shaping the autonomous rational individual, a condition of modern democracy. Electronic writing furthers all these features of handwriting and print simply because it is a far more efficient system of storage. Compared with print, digitized writing requires less time to copy and less space to store.

But electronic writing also subverts the culture of print.[11] In the case of word processing, the ease of altering digital writing, the immateriality of signs on the screen compared with ink on the page, shifts the text out of a register of fixity and into one of volatility. Also digital texts lend themselves to multiple authorship. Files may be exchanged between people in several ways, each person working on the text, with the result, in its spatial configuration on a screen or printed on paper, hiding any trace of signature. In addition, hypertext programs encourage the reader to treat the text as a field or network of signs in which to create his or her own linkages, linkages which may become part of the text and which other readers may follow or change at their will. These programs permit searches for words or phrases throughout a text or group of texts which may be added to the text or saved. The result is a new text which brings terms together that were not so associated by the author. The reader has substituted their own hierarchy of terms for that of the author. With electronic writing the distinction between author and reader collapses and a new form of text emerges that may challenge the canonicity of works, even the boundaries of disciplines.

Computer message services establish a form of communication that also subverts the culture of handwriting and print. There are several forms of these electronic "post offices." In the case of electronic mail, the individual has an "address" on a computer and anyone who knows it may send a message or letter to it from their own computer. In another instance, certain computers serve as "bulletin boards" which allow many individuals to browse through messages and leave their own. These "electronic cafes" encourage

strangers, individuals who have never met face to face, to communicate to one another. Strangers here exchange messages without the
extraneous presence of the body or the voice, only signs passing from
one to another. What is more, these bulletin boards use pseudonyms
or handles: individuals do not use their own names and may easily
disguise any of their attributes, such as gender or ethnicity. As a form
of writing, the message services foster not the autonomous, rational,
stable individual but the playful, imaginative multiple self. In coun-
tries that have experimented extensively with message services, such
as France, they have proven enormously popular.[12] People seem to
enjoy a communication technology in which they invent themselves in
the process of exchanging signs.

Another form of communication enabled by computer writing is
computer conferencing.[13] In this instance, digital writing substitutes
not for print but for face-to-face meetings and oral communications.
Computer conferences eliminate the need for gathering people in one
place at one time. There exists now an alternative to synchronous
meeting or community as we know it. A central computer reserves an
area for the conference. Individuals, using their personal computers
hooked up to telephones, call that computer and read the presenta-
tions and comments of others, responding as they see fit. Studies of
computer conferences reveal that the gain is not simply efficiency:
new qualities of community relations develop in this cyberspace.
Without the cues of body language, status, force of personality,
gender, clothing style – all present in face-to-face situations – conversation changes in character. Interventions are less conventional, less
deferential, as social authority is cancelled through computer writing.
Criteria for effective responses change to typing speed and terse
expression. Some analysts argue that computer conferencing creates
conditions for a form of democracy more vibrant and animated by
unorthodox thought than the colonial town meeting.[14] While this
form of computer writing may never fully replace traditional community, it offers an alternative to synchronous meeting that meliorates
the increasing isolation of the information age.

The theory of deconstruction of Jacques Derrida anticipates in
many ways changes brought about by computer writing.[15] He
counters the traditional theory of writing as fixity of meaning, monu-
mentality, the authority of the author by focusing on the material
aspect of signs inscribed on pages. He argues that such inscription
leaves language open to multiple meaning, that the spacing of traces
differs and displaces meaning away from the author, that the linear

form of the book, with its order of pagination, its margins, its diacritical markings, its chapters and paragraphs, imposes a hierarchy that the reader may subvert by taking it as a text, a stream of marks whose contradictions and impasses are open to a close reading. Western thought relies upon printed writing to support the author's stable meaning, to insist that the book signifies only what the author intended. This "logocentrism," as Derrida terms it, works by exclusions, supplements and marginalizations which may be reintroduced in a subversive reading. Books establish oppositions of terms, binaries in which one term is subordinate to the other and often absent from text. In the American Declaration of Independence the phrase "all men are created equal" omits women and suppresses the question of race, even as it inscribes these groups as inferior. Deconstruction attempts to destabilize the march of univocal meaning in written texts by unlocking the logic of difference that it hides.

Derrida's interpretive gesture is similar to my understanding of electronic writing. Both deconstruction and electronic writing understand the volatility of written language, its instability and uncertain authorship. Both see language as effecting a destabilization of the subject, a dispersal of the individual, a fracturing of the illusion of unity and fixity of the self. Derrida, however, understands these qualities of writing as applying to all of its forms and he differentiates only partially between handwriting, print and digital writing.[16] Deconstruction, then, is Derrida's interpretation of writing in all its forms. By contrast my effort is to distinguish between print and electronic forms of writing, to assess the significance of the difference enacted by a new communications technology. Derrida's strategy removes the task of interpretation from the context of contemporary changes in culture and society, repeating the gesture of earlier thinkers by producing a discourse as a reinterpretation. Ultimately, then, the force of deconstruction returns to see Derrida as a Western philosopher, defeating his own effort to subvert that position. Nonetheless the corpus of Derrida's writing provides powerful analytic tools to criticize the cultural and ideological patterns that have accompanied print writing. In that way, and to a certain extent, deconstruction permits the reading of texts in a manner that suits electronic writing.

In the examples of TV ads, databases and computer writing, poststructuralist perspectives enable a comprehension of the linguistic features of new communications technologies and relate these to the cultural problem of the constitution of the subject. In particular they enable us to see the way electronically mediated communication promotes a new configuration of the subject that may be termed postmodern in the sense that it is structurally different from that of the modern era. Research on the mode of information has barely begun and much remains to extend these analyses to communications technologies not even mentioned here. I want now to raise some epistemological and political issues concerning the use of poststructuralist theory in the field of communications and point to additional areas for further research.

The theory of mode of information intersects with critical social theory's recognition of the stalled dialectic. As the Frankfurt School recognized long ago, in the course of the twentieth century, working-class movements have attenuated, abated or disappeared altogether, interrupting or permanently suspending the dialectic of the class struggle. The critical social theory of the Frankfurt School and more generally Western Marxism interpreted this situation as the deleterious effect of mass culture on the proletariat. However, these theorists do not adequately conceptualize the role of electronically mediated communications in the cultural integration of the working class into modern society. A good part of their difficulty stems from a theoretical model that does not account, with regard to the phenomena of mass culture, for the constitution of the subject through language, more specifically through the language patterns of the mode of information. The theoretical tendency of Western Marxism has been to approach the question of a politically stabilized modernity from orientations themselves far too rooted in modernity and its communications technologies. Like modern thinkers since Descartes, they attempt to establish an atemporal or universal foundation for theory which usually takes the form of some definition of the human.

The grounding of theory in the human works to dehistoricize one's position, making it invulnerable to temporal contingency but also to render it blind to its dependence on that contingency. In the twentieth century, for example, communication has been dramatically altered by electronic technologies, a situation, as I argue above, that urges social theorists to look anew at many of their fundamental assumptions. The widespread dissemination of radio, telephone, film, television, computer-enhanced communications such as electronic mail and computer conferencing, telex and fax machines and satellite communications systems changes not only communications but basic features of social life. Whatever *theoretical* priority one wishes to place on the question of communications, when recent *historical* developments are taken into account, it must move from the periphery to the center of social science. But this means that the problem of communication theory begins with a recognition of necessary self-reflexivity, of the dependence of knowledge on its context. It requires from the outset a frank acknowledgement of contingency: the "truth" of communication theory is registered in relation to historical change and is in no sense "absolute," offering no vantage point from which one can claim a purchase on universality. A continuing issue for communication theory, then, is to sustain this sense of contingency, to develop strategies to avoid at every level and every turn becoming grounded, stabilized, founded, established in the Truth. Communication theory must then produce a new kind of truth, one not linked to the modernist goal of universality.

Because communication theory is so obviously and directly responding to the world with its unpredictable shifts and turns, the temptation is strong for theorists, at the epistemological level, to flee that world, to reduce that contingency, to find some stable ground upon which to secure a firm knowledge. Norbert Wiener's "cybernetic" theory of communication, to take one example, turned to mathematics for a ground, the traditional locus of pure theory, a theory that appears at least not to depend in any way on the vagaries of human time.[17] Communication knowledge for him becomes a precisely determinable ratio of information to noise. But an important lesson learned from the impact on social theory of the shift to electronically mediated communication is that theory must avoid the pretense that it is independent of the world, must protect itself at every point against slipping into the assumption that it is somehow constructed on a foundation of self-generated certainty. The first principle of communication theory in the age of electronic technology, then, is that there is no first principle, only a recognition of an outside of theory, an other to theory, a world that motivates theory.

The requirement that theoretical categories have built into them a certain contingency or self-limitation faces an equal difficulty from an opposite side, the side of history. The danger here is that history, once invoked to forestall abstract theorizing, itself becomes a stable, dogmatic ground. In this case the context provides the foundation for theory: a presumed certainty or closure within the context of theory "guarantees" its truth. The pertinent example in this case is Marxist writing on communications which takes the mode of production as a fixed horizon, focusing on questions that refer back to it (such as what is the effect of the corporate structure on the information age and vice versa) and omitting or repressing questions that do not appear to relate to the class structure. History in this perspective is already a given, and the new ingredient, in this case electronic communications, poses no new questions, merely reinforces old ones. For communication theory, the turn to history must sustain a sense of an open field, not a closed totality, a sensitivity to the new, not a confirmation of the already given.

Poststructuralist interpretive strategies are germane to communication theory because they attempt to confront both of these theoretical dilemmas. They make problematic both the authorial position of the theorist and the categories he or she develops. By focusing on language and stressing the instability of meaning in language, poststructuralist theory undermines the effort to dissolve communication into a "real" of action or into a universal definition of the human. At the same time it calls into question versions of the relation of theory and history/context which present the latter as a closed or totalized field that serves to turn theory into ideology, into a discourse whose assumptions are disavowed or made invisible.[18] For these reasons poststructuralist theory opens the field of electronically mediated communications in a way that locates its internal complexity and its relation to culture. It enables one to see what is new in the dissemination and emplacement of these technologies.

Poststructuralist theory is often accused of its own kind of totalization, linguistic reductionism. It is charged with never going beyond the text, of depoliticizing social action, of theorizing only an endless play of discourse analysis. While the practice of some poststructuralists may lend itself to this accusation, my effort, in theorizing the mode of information, has been to counteract the textualist tendency by linking poststructuralist theory with social change, by connecting it with electronic communications technology, by "applying" its methods to the arena of everyday life, by insisting on communications as a historical context which justifies the move to an emphasis on language. The "linguistic turn" of poststructuralism is apposite not only for its ability to critique modernist theory but because of changes in the socio-historical field. By the same token, I relate poststructuralist theory to the mode of information to underline the contingency of that theory, not to provide it with a false stability, a solid foundation in history. The political implications of the resort to poststructuralism, then, must be viewed in this light.

Poststructuralist theory invalidates modernist political positions, those that rely upon a view of humanity as in need of emancipation from forms of external oppression.[19] These views presuppose man as centered in rational autonomy but as prevented from attaining this center by institutions that block its realization: arbitrary government, religious intolerance, private appropriation of the means of production. However, the focus on language rejects this position because language already configures the individual. Only after the individual has been constituted as centered in rational autonomy by Enlightenment discourse does it appear that monarchy, institutional religion and capitalism are external fetters to freedom. If language is seen as already implicating the individual, then the question of emancipation changes its character. The question becomes one of understanding the positioning of the individual in the given language pattern and the relative change of altering that pattern, rather than one of a search for an absolute universal beyond the given order, one that would somehow allow an already defined human creature to emerge as if from its tutelage, or chains.

Contemporary society contains modernist institutions and discourses which privilege certain configurations of the subject, those that support autonomous rationality, and subordinate others (women, ethnic minorities, etc.). But contemporary society also contains "postmodernist" institutions and discourses, such as electronically mediated communications, which support new configurations of the subject. To the extent that it is now appropriate to raise the issue of the restrictions of modernist forms of subject constitution, electronic communications, understood in a poststructuralist sense, provide a basis for critique. This does not mean that every emission from such communications technology is automatically revolutionary; the great preponderance of these communications works to solidify existing society and culture. But there is a way of understanding their impact that reveals its potential for structural change. In other words, there is a secular trend emanating from electronic communications that undermines the stability of the figure of the rational autonomous individual. Hence the outcry against these communications, the warnings of their dangers by those adhering to modernist political positions.

The other tendency that amplifies the poststructuralist understanding of the political impact of electronic communications is the spread of protest movements from outside the modernist paradigm, certain feminist and ethnic positions, certain aspects of gay and lesbian politics, certain kinds of ecological and anti-nuclear concerns. To the extent that the politics of these groups challenges the privilege of the rational individual as the universal ground of human identity (the Western tradition), they effect changes that are parallel with those of electronic communications. The operation of hegemonic ideology is effective to the extent that it is unrecognized. When everyone assumes that human beings have a nature, centered in reason, that is violated by institutional chains, then those chains are exposed but that ideology is confirmed. Electronic communications and the social movements mentioned above sometimes tend to put modernist ideology into question, thereby changing the terms of political discussion. When this is effective, as in the effort to abandon the required teaching of Western Civilization as the exclusive introduction to culture, modernists of all stripes, from the Marxist Eugene Genovese to the conservative Lynn Chaney, recognize only a threat to freedom. To those not under the complete spell of this ideology, its operations become manifest and hence dissolved: "man" cannot mean Western man, rationality is not the final ground of human experience.

Electronically mediated communication opens the prospect of understanding the subject as constituted in historically concrete configurations of discourse and practice. It clears the way to seeing the self as multiple, changeable, fragmented, in short as making a project of its own constitution. In turn such a prospect challenges all those discourses and practices that would restrict this process, would fix and stabilize identity, whether these be fascist ones which rely on essentialist theories of race, liberal ones which rely on reason, or socialist ones which rely on labor. A poststructuralist understanding of new communications technologies raises the possibility of a postmodern culture and society that threatens authority as the definition of reality by the author.

5

Databases as Discourse, or Electronic Interpellations

I The Mode of Information and Databases

In this chapter I shall underscore the way computerized databases function as discourses in Foucault's sense of the term, that is, the way they constitute subjects outside the immediacy of consciousness.[1] This effort contrasts with other critical positions on databases which miss their discursive effects, treating databases with categories that overlook the decentering operations of language on the subject. Such, for example, is the case with Marxist writings, such as those of Herbert Schiller and Tim Luke,[2] in which databases are seen as contributions to the power of major institutions, especially corporations. Here databases are a new instrument for capitalists to tighten their grip on the mode of production. Information in databases, Marxist critics advise, are not equally available to all, as the somewhat utopian proponents of this technology contend, but redound preponderantly to the benefit of the economic ruling class. Similarly, liberal writers on the subject, such as David Burnham, James Rule and Gary Marx,[3] address in particular the appropriation of database technology by the state, warning of the considerable augmentation of centralized power it provides. Liberals are concerned in particular with the threats to privacy occasioned by databases in the hands of the government.

While these perspectives certainly offer much to consider, they fail to expose the cultural innovations brought about by the integration of database technology into existing political, economic and social institutions. In each case, Marxist and liberal perspectives incorporate the novel system of knowledge into their existing conceptual frameworks, revealing only that side of the phenomenon that fits within its grid of understanding. For Marxists, databases are comprehensible only to the extent they are a factor in the struggle over the means of production; for liberals, databases enter the field of politics as a component in the never-ending danger of autocratic central government. For both positions the novelty of databases is reduced to a minimum and the social individual or class as configured by the theory remains unchanged with the advent of the new. I posit that critical social theory must explore, in addition to these offerings, the relation of databases to the cultural issue of the constitution of the subject, and that to do so Foucault's theory of discourse provides a most compelling guide.

With respect to the problem of culture, the chief limitation of Marxist and liberal theories is that they configure the social field primarily as one of action, minimizing the importance of language. With respect to databases, the action in question for Marxists is the relation of power between capitalists and workers, while for liberals it is the fate of political domination. Both positions forget that databases are composed of symbols; they are in the first instance representations of something. One does not eat them, handle them, or kick them, at least one hopes not. Databases are configurations of language; the theoretical stance that engages them must at least take this ontological fact into account. A form of language, databases will have social effects that are appropriate to language, though certainly they will also have varied relations with forms of action as well.

The poststructuralist understanding of language is of special relevance to an analysis of databases that proceeds from critical social theory because of the connection it draws between language and the constitution of the subject. Poststructuralists make a number of salient claims about the interaction of language and subjects: (1) that subjects are always mediated by language; (2) that this mediation takes the form of "interpellation"; and (3) that in this process the subject position that is a point of enunciation and of address is never sutured or closed, but remains unstable, excessive, multiple.

The first proposition is to be understood neither as tautological nor as innocent. A human being is configured as a subject, is given cultural significance, in the first instance through language. The kind of bearing that society imposes on individuals, the nature of the constraint and the empowerment it operates takes its effect in language. The significance of the proposition may become more clear if we remember that in our culture the bearing of language on individuals tends to be systematically obscured by the privilege we give (in language) to the subject as a point of origin of motivation, consciousness and intention. Since Descartes' articulation of the configuration of the subject, since the dissemination of this configuration in Enlightenment thought, since the inscription of this configuration in the major institutions of representative democracy, capitalist economics, bureaucratic social organization and secular education, it has become the cultural foundation of the West. Once understood as a subject, the individual is fixed in the binary opposites of autonomy/ heteronomy, rationality/irrationality, freedom/determinism. The linguistic level of the configuration is actively forgotten or naturalized as the subject faces these binaries from the vantage point of interior consciousness.

At the micrological level of daily life the subject is continuously reconstituted as such through interpellation or "hailing."[4] In determinate linguistic acts the subject is addressed in a position and/or provoked to an enunciative stance in a manner that obscures the position or the stance. When a teacher calls upon an elementary-school student to answer a question, the position of the student as an autonomous rational agent is presupposed, a position that student must "stand into" first in order to be able to answer, in order to be a student. The operation of linguistic interpellation requires that the addressee accept its configuration as a subject without direct reflection in order to carry on the conversation or practice at hand. Interpellation may be calibrated by gender, age, ethnicity or class or may exclude any of these groups or parts of them. The issue is not that interpellation is an invasion of society upon the individual that ought to be avoided; that objection already falls within the binary freedom/determinism and presupposes the constitution of the individual as subject. Rather what is important is that the process goes on at the level of language and that in our culture it takes the particulur form of the subject.

The third proposition is that the interpellation of the subject is always partial, incomplete, riddled with gaps and open to reconfiguration and resistance. The constitution of the subject in language is different from the Newtonian understanding of the world of material objects in which matter is pushed and pulled into determinate positions by laws that are inexorable and unchanging. In the most trivial case, the subject is always multiple, interpellated into different positions: the student is also child, friend, pet, master. But in each instance of interpellation, the subject is configured as fixed, determinate, closed. In adult circumstances of some social weight, interpellation appears to be or, better, is structured as final, real, complete. The fixing of identities is not a matter of being pushed or pulled by gravity but of being invited to play a role in such a way that the invitation appears to have already been answered by the subject before it was proposed, but at the same time the invitation could be refused.

II   Foucault's Concept of Discourse

An understanding of the poststructuralist sense of the relation of language to the subject is necessary to gauge the stakes at play in Foucault's concept of discourse, a concept that in turn is crucial to a critical approach to databases. Foucault employs the term discourse in most of his writings, especially in his work of the 1960s, *The Order of Things* (1966) and *The Archaeology of Knowledge* (1969). In these works Foucault presented a critique of the human sciences and an alternative method of analysis. Here the term discourse is introduced above all as a counter-position to those who understand writing as the expression of a subject, those who, in their search for meaning in acts of reading or listening, move from words back to consciousness. Here is one of Foucault's more lucid statements of this position.

> In the proposed analysis, instead of referring back to *the* synthesis or *the* unifying function of *a* subject, the various enunciative modalities manifest his dispersion. To the various statuses, the various sites, the various positions that he can occupy or be given when making a discourse. To the discontinuity of the planes from which he speaks. . . . I shall abandon any attempt, therefore, to see discourse as a phenomenon of expression – the verbal translation of a previously established synthesis; instead, I shall look for a field of regularity for various positions of subjectivity. Thus conceived, discourse is not the majestically unfolding manifestation of a thinking, knowing, speaking subject, but, on the contrary, a totality, in which the dispersion of the subject and his discontinuity with himself may be determined. It is a space of exteriority in which a network of distinct sites is deployed.[5]

The relation of writing to the subject is sharply reconfigured in this passage. The term discourse is used primarily as a way to register the difference of Foucault's theory of writing from that of humanism. It designates a move toward an exteriorization of the analysis which itself is strategic. Foucault's claim is not that he has discovered the one, true way to understand knowledge or even that his way is somehow epistemologically superior to other, humanist ways. Only that if one seeks a critique of knowledge in our culture, if one seeks to distance oneself from our culture's way of regarding its own knowledge, the term discourse indicates the path of that move.

Many critics of Foucault, who are usually themselves within the humanist way of knowing, complain that Foucault does not adequately specify the term discourse as a field, does not carefully indicate the boundaries of discourse, or its object. Manfred Frank, for example, even quotes Foucault as acknowledging this deficiency, except Frank takes it as an admission of failure rather than as an indication that the interest of the term discourse lies not in relation to a well-defined object but in relation to a level of analysis of any knowledge domain. Here is Frank's quote from Foucault:

> Finally, instead of making the rather hazy meaning of the word "discourse" more distinct, I think that I have multiplied its meanings: sometimes using it to mean a general domain of all statements [énoncés], sometimes as an individualisable group of statements [énoncés], and sometimes as an ordered practice which takes account of a certain number of statements [énoncés].[6]

Foucault appears to be suggesting that, if the aim is a critique of knowledge in our society, then the effort of theorization need not so much focus on delimiting the object but on specifying the level of meaning one is attempting so that the relation of knowledge to the subject – in other words, the cultural construction of the subject – can be raised as a question.

Beginning with the essay "The Discourse on Language," first presented as his inaugural lecture at the Collège de France in 1970, Foucault introduced a connection between the terms discourse and power. From that point on, most effectively in *Discipline and Punish* and *The History of Sexuality*, Foucault developed usages of the category "discourse" that were distinct from those in his earlier works. In the 1970s and 1980s discourse was frequently used as a couplet, "discourse/practice," an indication that Foucault refused the separation of discourse from the "non-discursive." He also introduced terms such as "technology of power" and "micro-physics of power" in which discourse was subsumed into arrays and articulations of various kinds of practices, institutional, disciplinary, resistive and so forth. The question of the relation of language to the subject was here considerably broadened: as language, discourse was configured as a form of power and power was understood as operating in part through language.

III   The Panopticon as Discourse

The question of discourse, with its imbrication to power, then, is about the cultural issue of the constitution of the subject. And in particular it is about the constitution of the subject as a rational, autonomous individual. Max Weber had also developed the thesis of the rational subject as a problem, as an index of domination rather than, as in liberalism and to a certain extent in Marx, as a sign of freedom. But Weber's understanding of rationality was burdened by its character as a universal principle. He was able to historicize the problem of reason and the subject only to a minimal extent. Foucault noted this difference in his position from that of Weber, attributing to the latter an understanding of rationality as "an anthropological invariant," whereas Foucault's own effort was to analyze reason as historically constructed.[7]

Foucault's problem then is to construct a theory of discourse that historicizes reason, reveals the way discourse functions as power and spotlights the constitution of the subject. Strictly speaking Foucault never provided such a theory because, he argued, theory reinscribes the rational subject at another epistemological level. Instead he demonstrated such a theory of discourse in his histories of punishment and sexuality. The closest he approached such a theory is found in brief statements, mostly in his occasional writings, such as the following given in a late interview:

> I do indeed believe that there is no sovereign, founding subject, a universal form of subject to be found everywhere. I am very skeptical of this view of the subject and very hostile to it. I believe, on the contrary, that the subject is constituted through practices of subjection, or in a more autonomous way, through practices of liberation, of liberty, . . . on the basis, of course, of a number of rules, styles, inventions to be found in the cultural environment.[8]

Discourse is understood as having a power effect on the subject even in movements of "liberation."

The power effect of discourse is to position the subject in relation to structures of domination in such a way that those structures may *then* act upon him or her. The chief characteristic of the power effect of discourse is to disguise its constitutive function in relation to the subject, appearing only after the subject has been formed as an addressee of power. A classic example of this operation of discourse is, for Foucault, psychoanalysis. The discourse/practices of Freud produce in the subject an Oedipalized child, an understanding of one's childhood as, in the case of boys, a desire for one's mother. Once the child-subject is so constituted by psychoanalytic discourse, the child is then seen as being forbidden this desire, with the consequences of the Oedipal traumas and its deep effects on the personality. But the crucial point is that the effect of the discourse/practice is to name the child's desire, to configure the child as a libidinal subject with the particular aim of its mother.[9] Discourse has the same function in *Discipline and Punish*.

The modern system of punishment, incarceration, is first of all itself not the result of a rational subject. Against liberals and Marxists, Foucault argues for a Nietzschean genealogy of prisons in which its origins are found neither in the ideas of the Enlightenment nor in the workings of early industrial capitalism. Foucault traces the origins of the prison to a multiplicity of non-related pieces of earlier history: Enlightenment critiques of Ancien Régime forms of punishment, military training practices and schedules, procedures of examination in schools, Bentham's architectural ideas for prisons – none of which is understandable as a cause of the prison. Foucault attributes the origin of the prison to a kind of non-agency as follows: "Small acts of cunning endowed with a great power of diffusion, subtle arrangements, apparently innocent, but profoundly suspicious, mechanisms that obeyed economies too shameful to be acknowledged, or pursued petty forms of coercion – it was nevertheless they that brought about the mutation of the punitive system, at the threshold of the contemporary period."[10] Having dethroned the rational subject from the agency of the establishment of prisons, Foucault goes on to analyze its operations as discourse.

The story is by now well known. Prisoners reside in cells surrounding a central tower in which a guard is placed who can look into the cells but whom prisoners cannot see. A peculiar authority is thereby instituted, one who is all-seeing (hence the term "panopticon") but invisible. This instance is part of a complex articulation of discourse/ practices which includes the juridical practices that sentenced the individual to prison, criminologists who study prisoners as individual cases, administrative schedules and routines for prisoner activities, evaluation procedures for possible parole, and so forth. Foucault characterizes the operation of the panopticon in these words: "By means of surveillance, disciplinary power became an integrated system . . . it also organized as a multiple, automatic and anonymous power; for although surveillance rests on the individual, its functioning is that of a network of relations from top to bottom . . . and laterally . . . this network holds the whole together and traverses it in its entirety with effects of power that derive from one another: supervisor perpetually supervised . . ."[11] Properly understood the panopticon is not simply the guard in the tower but the entire discourse/practice that bears down on the prisoner, one that constitutes him or her as a criminal. The panopticon is the way the discourse/ practice of the prison works to constitute the subject as a criminal and to normalize him or her to a process of transformation/rehabilitation. My argument is that, with the advent of computerized databases, a new discourse/practice operates in the social field, a super-panopticon if you will, which reconfigures the constitution of the subject.[12]

IV Databases as a Super-panopticon

Databases are discourse, in the first instance, because they effect a constitution of the subject. They are a form of writing, of inscribing symbolic traces, that extends the basic principle of writing as *différance*, as making different and as distancing, differing, putting off to what must be its ultimate realization. In its electronic and digital form, the database is perfectly transferable in space, indefinitely preservable in time; it may last forever everywhere. Unlike spoken language, the database is not only remote from any authorial presence but is "authored" by so many hands that it makes a mockery of the principle of author as authority. As a meaningful text, the database is no one's and everyone's yet it "belongs" to someone, to the social institution that "owns" it as property, to the corporation, the state, the military, the hospital, the library, the university. The database is a discourse of pure writing that directly amplifies the power of its owner/user.

Everyone knows this. Because they know it, they resist it. A poll by *Time* magazine in late 1991 revealed that between 70 and 80 percent of respondents were "very/somewhat concerned" about the amount of information being collected about them in databases, with the higher figure referring to the federal government, credit organizations and insurance companies and the lower figure referring to employers, banks and marketing companies.[13] The population is now cognizant of being surveilled constantly by databases and it apparently feels ill at ease as a result. Database anxiety has not of yet developed into an issue of national political prominence but it is clearly a growing concern of many and bespeaks a new level of what Foucault calls the normalization of the population.

Examples of the politicization of databases multiply every day. The federal government has developed FinCen (Financial Crimes Enforcement Network) with an awesome power that combines artificial intelligence programs with massive parallel processing to monitor bank transactions for the purpose of detecting criminal activity.[14] In the economic sphere, retailers that sell by modem regard the information they accumulate about customers as their property, as a valuable asset, gained as a by-product of the sale, which they may then sell to other retailers. But customers do not want such information about themselves travelling, beyond their ken, from one vendor to another. Although an effort in the early 1990s to sell customer information by the Lotus corporation was thwarted by consumer protests,[15] resistance to the use of these types of database is likely to fail because it is based on the modern, political distinction between the public and the private. Consumers regard their purchases as private, as part of the capitalist system which designates all economic transactions as "private." But databases are a postmodern discourse that traverse and cancel the public/private distinction.

Increasingly economic transactions automatically enter databases and do so with the customer's assistance. Credit card sales are of course good examples. According to the conventional wisdom of political economy, the consumer buys something in a "private" act of rational choice. Yet when the credit card is extracted from the wallet or purse and submitted to the clerk for payment, that "private" act has become part of a "public" record. The unwanted surveillance of one's personal choice becomes a discursive reality through the willing participation of the surveilled individual. In this instance the play of power and discourse is uniquely configured. The one being surveilled provides the information necessary for the surveillance. No carefully designed edifice is needed, no science like criminology is employed, no complex administrative apparatus is invoked, no bureaucratic organization need be formed. In the super-panopticon, surveillance is assured when the act of the individual is communicated by telephone line to the computerized database, with only a minimal amount of data being entered by the sales clerk. A gigantic and sleek operation is effected whose political force of surveillance is occluded in the willing participation of the victim.

Unlike the panopticon, then, the super-panopticon effects its workings almost without effort. What Foucault notices as the "capillary" extension of power throughout the space of disciplinary society is much more perfected today. The phone cables and electric circuitry that minutely crisscross and envelop our world are the extremities of the super-panopticon, transforming our acts into an extensive discourse of surveillance, our private behaviors into public announcements, our individual deeds into collective language. Individuals are plugged into the circuits of their own panoptic control, making a mockery of theories of social action, such as Weber's, which privilege consciousness as the basis of self-interpretation, and liberals generally, who locate meaning in the intimate, subjective recesses behind the shield of the skin. The individual subject is interpellated by the super-panopticon through technologies of power, through the discourse of databases that have very little if anything to do with "modern" conceptions of rational autonomy. For the super-panopticon, this perfect writing machine, constitutes subjects as decentered from their ideologically determined unity.

If we look at databases as an example of Foucault's notion of discourse we see them as "exteriorities," not as constituted by agents, and we look for their "rules of formation" as the key to the way they constitute individuals. Databases in this sense are carefully arranged lists, digitalized to take advantage of the electronic speed of computers. The list is partitioned vertically into "fields" for items such as name, address, age and sex and horizontally into "records" which designate each entry. A retailer's database has fields which record each purchase an individual makes so that in the course of time a rich portrait of buying habits is created, one that is instantaneously accessible and cross-referenced with other information such as the individual's location, and possibly cross-referenced as well with other databases keyed to items such as social security number or driver's licence. In effect these electronic lists become additional social identities as each individual is constituted for the computer, depending on the database in question, as a social agent. Without referring the database back to its owner and his or her interests or forward to the individual in question as a model of its adequacy or accuracy, we comprehend the database as a discursive production which inscribes positionalities of subjects according to its rules of formation. In this way we see the database outside the dichotomy public/private and outside the dynamics of the mode of production. Instead the discourse of the database is a cultural force which operates in a mechanism of subject constitution that refutes the hegemonic principle of the subject as centered, rational and autonomous. For now, through the database alone, the subject has been multiplied and decentered, capable of being acted upon by computers at many social locations without the least awareness by the individual concerned yet just as surely as if the individual were present somehow inside the computer.

Some readers may object that databases cannot be characterized as discourses in Foucault's sense, since for Foucault discourses were large collections of texts. The examples he gives are psychology, economics, grammar and medicine, all of which include sentences and paragraphs strung together by arguments. The same can hardly be said of databases, which for the most part are not textual in this way but rather agglomerations of isolated words or numbers whose location in the "discourse" are paramount. The only places where sentences of any kind are found in databases is in the program or code language that constitutes them and in some types of fields that are textual. And yet the crucial features of discourse are indeed contained in databases even though they omit the standard features of prose. Databases are fully what Foucault calls "grids of specification," one of the three "rules of formation" of discourse. These grids are "the systems according to which the different kinds of [the object in question] are divided, contrasted, related, regrouped, classified, derived from one another as objects of . . . discourse . . ." (*Archaeology*, 42). Nothing qualifies as a grid in this sense as well as databases; they are pure grids whose vertical fields and horizontal records divide and classify objects with a precision that more traditional forms of discourse such as psychology must surely envy.

But what is most important about discourses for Foucault is that they constitute their objects. His greatest concern is to avoid treating discourse as "groups of signs," as texts or as writing perhaps in Derrida's sense, "but as practices that systematically form the objects of which they speak" (*Archaeology*, 49). His emphasis is on the performative aspect of language, of what language does rather than what it denotes or connotes. Computerized databases are nothing but performative machines, engines for producing retrievable identities. A feature of many databases that indicates their status as "practice" is their "relational" abilities. Two databases may function as one if one field in each is identical. Thus if a census database and an employee database both have fields for social security numbers (which is increasingly the identifier field of choice), the employer may use the census to discover whatever he might about the employee that is not in his own records but in the census. These kinds of linkages between databases have been used in the Parent Locator System, the effort to find divorced and separated men who do not support their children. Relational databases thus have built into their structure the ability to combine with other databases, forming vast stores of information that constitute as an object virtually every individual in society and in principle may contain virtually everything recorded about that individual – credit rating data, military records, census information, educational experience, telephone calls, and so forth.[16]

The most sophisticated examples of the use of relational databases are in market research firms such as Claritas Corporation. This company boasts the use of "over 500 million individual consumer records from *several* leading databases."[17] The company combines and analyzes data from the following categories of databases: media and market research studies, newspaper research (including readership of newspapers, viewing of television and listening to radio), customer research studies, car and truck registration data, mailing lists and credit rating data. The company combines over 1,200 databases of both the private and public sectors. Claritas generates its own database, "compass," which it makes available to its customers for their own research. Its masterpiece, though, is a database called "prizm" that is an identity construction system. Prizm divides up the entire population into "clusters" which can be as fine grained as six households. Each cluster is then fit into forty types such as "rank and file," "black enterprise," "single city blues," "furs and station wagons," and so forth. Each type is defined by income, percentage of the US population, age, class, size of household, and "characteristics." In the case of the identity known as "bohemian mix," some 1.1 percent of the population, characteristics are, for example, "Buy, wine by the case, common stock; Drive, Alfa Romeos, Peugeots; Read, *GQ*, *Harper's*; Eat, whole-wheat bread, frozen waffles; TV, *Nightline* . . ." The company then provides a few sample zip codes where this species may be found.[18]

Databases such as prizm constitute subjects in a manner that inscribes a new pattern of interpellation.[19] The "hailing" of the individual is here quite distinct from that of the teacher and the student, the policeman and the perpetrator, the boss and the worker, the parent and the child. In these cases there is often a direct message sent and received in a face-to-face situation. With databases, most often, the individual is constituted in absentia, only indirect evidence such as junk mail testifying to the event. Interpellation by database in this respect is closer to the instance of writing, with the reader-subject being hailed by an absent author. But here again there are important differences: from the standpoint of the person being interpellated, the writer is known, even if only as a writer, and is an individual or finite group of individuals. The reader very often intentionally selects to be interpellated by the particular author, whereas in the example of computer databases that is rarely if ever the case. Interpellation by database is a complicated configuration of unconsciousness, indirection, automation, and absent-mindedness both on the part of the producer of the database and on the part of the individual subject being constituted by it. More research needs to be done in order to specify the configuration of interpellation in various types of databases, to answer the question of just how centered or dispersed subjects are in these cases and the characteristics of this dispersion or mutiplicity. However, the above discussion suffices to indicate the importance of databases in complicating the concept of interpellation. The computer database inaugurates a new era of interpellation far different from that of modernity with its discourses of print and its handwritten system of case files. The category of interpellation may serve as the leading thread in a critical interpretation of databases, one that specifies the attributes of subject constitution, reveals the domination inherent in the process, and indicates the path by which the positions of enunciation at which subjects are interpellated may be multiplied throughout social space, mollifying the noxious effects of the discourse.

Once the form of representation embodied in the database is understood, it may be compared with other regions of the mode of information – television viewing, computer writing, telephone conversation, video and audio recording, and so forth. Each of these cultural technologies also has discursive effects, the sum of which may be seen as slowly erecting the basis of a culture that is decidedly different from the modern. In each case the subject as coherent, stable, rational center is refuted by heterogeneity, dispersion, instability, multiplicity. The database is part of a larger, massive cultural transformation which positions the subject outside the framework of visibility available to liberal and Marxist theoretical orientations. No wonder Lyotard struck a chord when he announced in *The Postmodern Condition* his "incredulity toward metanarratives." As daily life is pervaded more and more by the regions of the mode of information, the culture of modernity enjoys less and less verisimilitude. Though the effects of the mode of information are differential with respect to class, gender and ethnicity, they constitute a very general phenomenon that betokens a new play of power, a new dialectics of resistance and a new configuration of politics and its theorization.

Like television, music reproduction, computer writing and video art, databases generate discursive effects by simulating a reality, or, better, to use Baudrillard's term, a hyper-reality. The fields that compose the database construct representations of individuals. The fields, often consisting of a fixed amount of characters, are highly limited by the imperative of the technology, its rule of formation in Foucault's sense, which is retrieval speed. The database is effective only to the extent that its information is instantaneously accessible, but at the same time it must be large and comprehensive in relation to its referent population. Near total coverage and instantaneous accessibility characterize a good database. Yet this accessibility refers to the constructions within the database, which function as simulacra of the population covered. To the database, Joe Jones is the sum of the information in the fields of the record that applies to that name. So the person Joe Jones now has a new form of presence, a new subject position that defines him for all those agencies and individuals who have access to the database. The representation in the discourse of the database constitutes the subject, Joe Jones, in highly caricatured yet immediately available form.

Another way of understanding the discursive nature of databases is to relate them to what Foucault calls governmentality. This is a form of power characteristic of welfare states. It is neither the microphysics of power that characterizes local situations in everyday life, nor the grand state power of monarchs and presidents. Governmentality is a kind of bureaucratic power, one that relies upon knowledge of the populace to police society and maintain order. Foucault in places calls it "biopower" and takes as its precursor the management of the family as in ancient Greece, the original meaning of economy.[20] He defines governmentality as follows: "To govern a state will therefore mean to apply economy, to set up an economy at the level of the entire state, which means exercising towards its inhabitants, and the wealth and behaviour of each and all, a form of surveillance and control as attentive as that of the head of a family over his household and goods."[21] Governmentality, or the form of power of the welfare states of the advanced industrial societies of the later twentieth century, is inconceivable without databases. The vast populations of these societies might well be ungovernable without databases. Databases provide contemporary governments with vast stores of accessible information about the population which facilitates the fashioning of policies that maintain stability. An important political effect of databases, as they have been disseminated in our societies, is to promote the "governmental" form of power, to make knowledge of the population available to coercive institutions at every level.

To counter this stabilizing effect of databases, Lyotard, in *The Postmodern Condition*, suggests that a new emancipatory politics would consist in giving everyone access to databases.[22] Certainly this policy, however utopian under present circumstances, would serve to democratize information. Each individual or group would have easy computer access to the same information as the government. Although such a prospect seems unlikely, given the increasing poverty in this country, it is conceivable that at least in principle computer access to such databases could be widely extended to the vast majority of the population. A policy that worked in this direction would indeed constitute a "freedom of information" act. The thought of government critics being able to race through the cyberspace of data even as it is recorded is a counterfactual that gives one pause.

Yet as a strategy of resistance it does not take into account the performative effect of the discourse of databases, their ability to constitute subjects. The implication of Lyotard's position is that "real" subjects would recuperate the "power" inherent in the databases, enabling them to manipulate its knowledge for their own ends, a politics different from the current conservative restrictions on the use of databases to those who can foot the bill, usually large social organizations. The thesis of the liberation of the databases presupposes the social figure of the centered, autonomous subject that the databases preclude. Postmodern culture configures multiple, dispersed subject positions whose domination is no longer effected by alienated power but by entirely new articulations of technologies of power. The cultural function of databases is not so much the institution of dominant power structures against the individual but in restructuring the nature of the individual. Lyotard's suggestion presumes that knowledge and power are separable, that increased availability of databases equals increased knowledge equals increased power. But the viewpoint that I am proposing posits a different relation of knowledge and power, one in which knowledge itself is a form of linguistic power, the culturally formative power of subject constitution.

The process of subject formation in the discourse of databases operates very differently from the panopticon. Foucault argued that the subjects constituted by the panopticon were the modern, "interiorized" individual, the one who was conscious of his or her own self-determination. The process of subject constitution was one of "subjectification," of producing individuals with a (false) sense of their own interiority. With the super-panopticon, on the contrary, subject constitution takes an opposing course of "objectification," of producing individuals with dispersed identities, identities of which the individuals might not even be aware. The scandal, perhaps, of the super-panopticon is its flagrant violation of the great principle of the modern individual, of its centered, "subjectified" interiority.

A politics of databases, then, would respond to the cultural form of subjectification in postmodernity. Instead of developing a resistant politics of privacy to counter the alleged incursions of databases on the autonomous individual, we need to understand the forms of agency appropriate to a dispersed, multiple subject and to generate strategies of resistance appropriate to that identity formation. The issue is not that the new forms of subjectification are in themselves emancipatory but that they are the new arena of contestation. A politics that circumscribes freedom around the skin of the individual, labelling everything inside private and untouchable, badly misconceives the present-day situation of digitized, electronic communications. Since our bodies are hooked into the networks, the databases, the information highways, they no longer provide a refuge from observation or a bastion around which one can draw a line of resistance. The road to greater emancipation must wend its way through the subject formations of the mode of information, not through those of an earlier era of modernity and its rapidly disappearing culture. The appeal for community, as Ernesto Laclau and Chantal Mouffe argue,[23] must take into account the forms of identity and communication in the mode of information, and resist nostalgia for the face-to-face intimacy of the ancient Greek agora. In the era of cyborgs, cyberspace and virtual realities, the face of community is not discerned easily through the mists of history, however materialist and dialectical it may be.

6

Critical Theory and TechnoCulture: Habermas and Baudrillard

Since World War II Marxist theory has confronted a conjuncture that has proven increasingly recalcitrant to its categories and analysis. Although the mode of production has remained capitalist, and therefore amenable to the critique of political economy, the locus of revolution and social protest has, within the most advanced capitalist nations, shifted further and further away from the labor process. In the period 1840 to 1880, when Marx searched the world panorama for signs of emancipatory stirrings, his eyes fixed on the English, French and German factory workers, the proletariat that resisted the harsh discipline of the new labor process. His hopes for the transformation of civil society lay with a class that was becoming or was sure to become the most numerous, the most downtrodden, the most exploited but at the same time the most necessary to modern capitalism.

Marx tended to overlook or at least to downplay the more ambiguous features of the situation. The most militant rebels came from two groups that were in transition: the artisans who were losing their independence as they moved into the factories; and the peasants, who came to the factories from the countryside, a world apart from the industrializing cities. The fact that these groups may have resisted capitalism because of the change in habits it demanded of them rather than because of its intrinsic structure was not highlighted in Marx's thinking. He attributed the revolutionary role of the proletariat to the exploitative structure of the capitalist labor process itself, which progressively impoverished the life circumstances of the workers. For Marx, the impetus to rebel against the new system came directly from the new system; the only response possible for the workers was to liberate themselves and the world from the conditions of wage labor. As the century wore on and workers' discontent took the form of political parties and labor unions that sought to ameliorate life within the system rather than to overturn it, Marx failed to account adequately for the possibility of cooptation.[1]

Historians have posited numerous explanations for the apparent domestication (temporary?) of the working class: better wages, stratification of the labor force, ethnic and regional differences, poor leadership at the party and union levels, changes in the liberal state, and nationalism, among others. Whatever the reason, the industrial working class no longer appeared, by the mid-twentieth century, the standard bearer of revolt. At the same time, other groups rose to prominence as centers of revolution. First the peasants of the third world, and more recently students, racial and ethnic minorities, women, gays, prisoners and environmentalists have all made legitimate claims as "proletarians," as the group most oppressed by society and most opposed to its continuation in its present form, and thus as the "revolutionary subject."

Many theoretical questions are posed to Marxism by the shifts in the locus of militancy, but there is one in particular I will address in these pages: did Marx adequately conceptualize the relationship between technology and culture, practice and consciousness, labor and symbolic interaction? It can be argued that Marx's faith in the revolutionary potential of the industrial working class was gained too easily, that he assumed too readily that material hardship and social subjugation were sufficient conditions for revolt. One finds numerous instances in his texts in which the connection between material conditions and communicational practice is drawn too closely. Given a certain structure of work, his writings contend, social agents are expected to produce a certain political outcome.

The issue at stake is not one of the neglect of ideas. In the first thesis on Feuerbach, Marx indicates that he is fully cognizant of the active role of ideas in history, of the subject as an intentional agent: "[I]n opposition to materialism, the *active* side was developed by idealism."[2] In addition, historical materialism specified a prominent role for ideology in the process of social analysis. Religious doctrines and political programs are, in Marx's historical writings, fundamental aspects of the class struggle. The difficulty in Marxist theory is not that consciousness is relegated to the backstage of the historical drama but that the categorial richness and articulation of Marxism subsumes the problems of culture to those of technology. The gap in Marxist theory may be one not of basic principle but of secondary theoretical elaboration. The analysis in Marx of the region of the workplace is subtle, differentiated, complex; the analysis of the culture of the workers is undeveloped and deficient in analytic specification. The critique of political economy explores every turn of the capitalist structure; the critique of cultural politics is general, vague, undeveloped.

The result of this uneven theoretical development is that Marxists have focused in great detail on what the workers did: how they worked, what they were paid, what conditions were responsible for their misery, how these changed, and how they could have changed. But there has been very little Marxist analysis of the impact of bourgeois ideas and practices upon their lives and political activities; about the way the structure of the workplace facilitated or retarded their communication, about the way the worker's relations with his or her community, spouse, children, relatives and friends influenced his or her choices and goals.[3]

Marxism provides a coherent general outline of a democratic workplace: the reorganization of labor will eliminate specific deficiencies in the capitalist factory. Whatever conundrums remain concerning the conflict between central planning and worker self-management, between consumer and producer interests, between the requirements of production and the ecological balance with nature, these are, for Marx and for most Marxists, secondary problems that can be resolved at the level of practice. Another set of questions is not so easily manageable: what forms of culture are consistent with socialist society? Does the transformation of the technological and social apparatus imply a change in the form of symbolic interaction? Are the meanings associated with capitalist production a target of political strategy?

Because Marx assumed that oppression stimulated the worker to contest capitalism he did not theorize extensively about the problems of revolutionary consciousness, language, and symbolic interaction or culture in general. Hence when the socio-political developments of the twentieth century did not follow the Marxist trajectory, the framework of historical materialism was put in doubt. The cloth of

Marxist theory becomes unraveled as new political movements pull at the threads of the concept of the mode of production. Marxism appears unable to account for today's oppositional movements: the Kurds of Iran, the Muslims of Bosnia, the prisoners and prostitutes of France, the women and blacks in the United States, the Basques of Spain and Quebecois of Canada, the ecologists of Germany, the youth of Britain. If Marxism is to survive as the critical theory of advanced capitalism it must become more than the special theory of the (male) workers' exploitation.

These complaints about Marxist theory cannot be answered with a simple phrase. It will not suffice to follow the example of Stalin and decide by fiat that language must be promoted from the superstructure to the base. Nor can one call for an eclectic expansion of the Marxist paradigm, adding where required some Kant or Weber or Freud. Experiments in this direction have foundered when diverse concepts rub uncomfortably against one another, generating electrostatic sparks rather than theoretical light.[4] Yet there have been substantial efforts by theorists to conceptualize anew the relation of technology and culture within a somewhat revised and loosened Marxist framework. In particular the work of Jürgen Habermas in Germany and Jean Baudrillard in France has had far-reaching impact on the revival of critical theory.

In the rethinking of Marxism by Habermas and Baudrillard, the common intellectual denominator is the importance given to language as the mediator between technology and culture. In the twentieth century there has arisen a profusion of theories of language upon which to draw: Saussure's structural linguistics, Wittgenstein's theory of language games, the Russian School's formalist linguistics, Bertalanffy's information theory, Searle's theory of speech acts, Bateson's systems theory of communication, Barthes' semiology, Chomsky's theory of generative grammar, Gadamer's hermeneutics, Foucault's analysis of discourse, Derrida's method of deconstruction, Lyotard's philosophy of phrases, and other forms of language analysis.

This far from complete list serves to remind one of the variety and richness of recent meditations on language. Given the prominence of the question of language, it is truly surprising that so little effort has been made to account for it: why should so much attention be given to language theory in the twentieth century, especially since World War II?[5] One possibility is that language has become more central to social practice. The relation of computer language to the brain, the diffusion of electronic media bringing discourse from around the world into the home, and the spread of bureaucracy through which politics and work rely more than ever on written forms of communication are all examples of new practices that drastically extend the role of language in everyday life. And one may argue that language is not so much central to social practice but that it is changing its character as it takes on electronic forms, that the way language solicits a subject, the way discourse constitutes positions of subjectivity, is undergoing drastic transformations. In another work I have termed this process the mode of information.[6]

In any case, for the purposes of this chapter it need only be acknowledged that philosophies of language present a challenge to the critical theory of society. For there is a tendency to argue, explicitly or implicitly, that language is prior to or formative of society itself. This position of course cannot be embraced by critical social theorists because it unduly restricts the scope of social theory and often illegitimately constricts the range of possible emancipation from domination. Habermas and Baudrillard, in very different ways, have wrestled with the question of language, subordinating it to and integrating it with critical social theory. In the process they have opened new perspectives on the relation of technology and culture, offering resolutions to the deficiencies of classical Marxism.

I

In the case of Habermas the shift toward language theory began in his 1968 essay "Technology and Science as 'Ideology,'" in which the Marxist notion of work came under attack.[7] Associated with the Frankfurt School, Habermas was extending a line of thought initiated by Max Horkheimer and Theodor Adorno in *Dialectic of Enlightenment* (1944). In that book Horkheimer and Adorno attempted to differentiate critical theory from the scientific tradition in which Marx and Engels had initiated it.[8] For Horkheimer and Adorno scientific rationality was a means of dominating nature that had also become a means of dominating men. If Enlightenment, from the Greeks to the *philosophes* of the eighteenth century, based its critique of social domination on reason and science, it sustained and nurtured domination in a different form, one that would under capitalism become the source for an insidious form of social domination.

Horkheimer and Adorno pleaded for a radical critique of the culture of capitalism rooted not in the workplace but in the legitimating ideology of science. Their experience of German fascism, in which political domination and scientific culture operated in harmony, resulted in their pessimism about the future of the class struggle and even in the efficacy of critical theory.

Far less disturbed by the gloomy events of the twentieth century than Horkheimer and Adorno, Habermas searched for a renewal of radical theory in the critique of science and technology. He traced a line of filiation between Marx's theory of labor and the conservative function of science:

> At the stage of their scientific-technical development . . . the forces of production appear to enter a new constellation with the relations of production. Now they no longer function as the basis of a critique of prevailing legitimations in the interest of political enlightenment, but become instead the basis of legitimation.[9]

The conservative alliance of science and class relations was rooted in structural changes in advanced capitalism. While Horkheimer, Adorno and even Marcuse stressed the negative prospects implied by these developments, Habermas took them as a sign of an inadequacy in Marx's critical theory. Marx was unable to present a critical evaluation of the legitimating role of science and technology because his theory did not distinguish clearly enough between emancipatory action and technique. Marx could not offer an "alternative to existing technology" because, Habermas thought, his theory of labor was itself scientistic and technical.

Habermas found a way out of the dilemma in a most surprising fashion. The political aims of critical theory were in jeopardy because it had discovered a connection between technology and culture. Technology had become a source of ideology; the successes of the production system transformed it into its own justification; matter was transmuted into ideas. This conundrum of critical theory was reversed by Habermas, who located in Max Weber's theory of action the basis for once again separating technology and culture. Weber distinguished between purposive-rational action and value-rational action, a dichotomy that Habermas employed to develop an antinomy between technical action and symbolic interaction. Marx's theory of labor praxis was limited to the former; the ends of social action were given; the means were geared to produce results in the technically most efficient manner. What was left out or sub-ordinated in Marx's account of work was language, communication, the means through which individuals recognized each other as sub-jects. Hence Marx was unable to distinguish between science and emancipation.

The problem with Habermas's double theory of action is that it is not properly grounded in critical theory. The new category is simply added on to the old with no theoretical elaboration, no "transcenden-tal deduction." Thus Habermas writes, "I shall take as my starting point the fundamental distinction between *work* and *interaction*."[10] But this "fundamental distinction" is neither self-evidently fundamen-tal nor an obvious starting point of argumentation. It is instead a conclusion, one that leads to an improper separation of technology and culture. The borrowing of the concept of symbolic interaction from Weber is not enough. It does not explore systematically the metaphysical presuppositions behind Weber's thought and it intro-duces an artificial, even arbitrary distinction which sets Habermas's thought down a wandering path into the thickets of the notion of the ideal speech situation. Eventually, in *The Theory of Communicative Action*,[11] Habermas will have to reintroduce a transcendental subject that directs his thought not beyond Marx but behind him, back to Kant. Faced with the dilemma of science as ideology, Habermas might have inquired into the difficulties in the notion of a rational subject and in that way avoided the subjectivism into which he eventually fell.

Habermas treats the question of language theory as an aspect of critical social theory. He rejects in turn (1) Chomsky's theory of generative grammar, since that grounds language in an asocial notion of human nature; (2) Saussurean linguistics, since that removes the study of language from active social subjects and treats it as a purely formal, objective phenomenon; and (3) Austin's speech act theory, since that provides no basis to evaluate critically the situation of the speaker. To account for language or symbolic interaction from the point of view of critical social theory, Habermas develops the notion of the ideal speech situation. Speech is an effort to communicate and this for Habermas necessarily implies that what the speaker says is comprehensible, that what the speaker states is true, that the speaker is sincere, and that the utterance fits into a normative context. On the basis of these criteria language becomes available for analysis in terms of the distortions introduced into speech by social modes of domination.

Habermas is aware that few if any conversations meet the criteria of the ideal speech situation. Nevertheless, he argues for the apodicticity of his concept: "No matter how the intersubjectivity of mutual understanding may be deformed, the design of an ideal speech situation is necessarily implied with the structure of potential speech; for every speech, even that of intentional deception, is oriented towards the idea of truth."[12] In other words, "truth, freedom and justice" are inseparable tools of linguistic analysis. Habermas is maintaining, in a somewhat Kantian manner, that the ideal speech situation is a necessary condition for the comprehension of any utterance. The degree to which speech fails to meet the criteria of the ideal speech situation signifies not an individual's failure to communicate but social oppression, ultimately the class struggle.

There are many difficulties with the notion of the ideal speech situation. To begin with, one might ask if it is possible to evaluate empirically a given conversation according to Habermas's criteria. In the flow of interchanges between a husband and a wife, as represented imaginatively, for example, in *Who's Afraid of Virginia Woolf*, the levels of distortion are so complex that untangling "the truth" and analyzing the structures of domination might be impossible. In fact, the concept of the ideal speech situation implies a God-like epistemological vantage point from which the foibles of everyday confusions could be sorted out. But let us set aside the empirical problems and agree with Habermas that deviations from the ideal speech situation "increase correspondingly to the varying degrees of repression which characterize the institutional system within a given society; and that, in turn, the degree of repression depends on the developmental stage of the productive forces and on the organization of authority . . ."[13] If that is so, another difficulty arises: the analysis of symbolic interaction remains a direct reflection of the mode of production and we are back to where we began, with the problem of labor.

Habermas sought to extract the notion of the ideal speech situation from the grip of the economic structure by arguing that "communicative competence" is itself a historical phenomenon. The ability of speakers to meet the ideal criteria thus depends not only on the levels of repression introduced by the mode of production but on the stage of "moral development" of the individual. Communication is depicted as an evolutionary phenomenon in its own right, one that depends on issues of socialization and personality development.

Habermas contends that "the species learns not only in the dimension of technically useful knowledge decisive for the development of productive forces but also in the dimension of moral-practical consciousness decisive for structures of interaction."[14] Just as there is progress in the evolution of modes of production, so there are criteria, provided for the most part by Piaget, by which to evaluate communicative competence. During stage one an "imperativist mode of communication" is predominant; there ensues the era of "propositionally differentiated speech"; finally we arrive at an epoch, presumably our own, in which speech is "argumentative" and fully subject to the criteria of the ideal speech situation. Changes from one stage to the next are made possible, according to Habermas, by general changes in social organization.[15] The implication of Habermas's argument is that in the next stage of social organization, the one beyond capitalism or a more democratic stage within capitalism, communicative competence will enable and social freedom will authorize the realization of the ideal speech situation. This position has led Habermas, to the chagrin of the radical left in Germany,[16] to argue for a "public sphere" in which open debate would provide the conditions for qualitative social change.

The utopianism of Habermas's political position is rooted in the subjectivism of his theory. If speech is distorted systematically by social repression it is not likely that open debate in the public sphere would eliminate that distortion. Such an ideal speech situation would still be subject to the general forms of repression. Even in the context of "the legitimation crisis" it is difficult to see how the distortions can be eliminated, for Habermas's version of critical theory depends upon an unjustified view of the subject as "ideally" truthful. But the pressure to be truthful does not necessarily produce the truth; it might just as well lead to more elaborate lies or self-deceptions. In the end Habermas's theory leads to a demand for an ideal speech situation which is not adequately based on an analysis of the structure of communication in everyday life. To attain that sort of analysis one must posit language as an objective phenomenon, at least provisionally, and carry out an investigation of it that renders it intelligible socially and historically. This is the direction of the work of Jean Baudrillard, who frees critical theory from an unwarranted dependence on evaluating the subjectivity of social participants by which, as we have seen, the analysis of culture is divorced from that of technology.

II

Baudrillard's early works *Le Système des objets* (1968) and *La Société de consommation* (1970) took their inspiration from the problematics of the critique of everyday life developed by Baudrillard's teacher Henri Lefebvre and from Roland Barthes' semiology.[17] Under advanced capitalism, Baudrillard maintained, consumerism had come to dominate the various aspects of everyday life. At this stage of his thinking Baudrillard was happy to place the regional analysis of consumption within the broader Marxist critique of capitalism. The experience of the events of May 1968 had dramatized changes in the structure of capitalism, such as the importance of everyday life, that required analysis and critique. Where Baudrillard differed from traditional Marxism was in his use of semiological theory[18] to make intelligible in a new way the features of consumerism.

Like Habermas, Baudrillard was unwilling to accept language theory – in this case structuralist semiology – in its dominant versions. Saussure's structural linguistics, as employed by Lévi-Strauss, Lacan and Barthes, enables the investigator to examine phenomena at a new level of complexity. An object can be dissected into its binary oppositions, revealing a play of rules and patterns of formation, without resorting to a concept of consciousness or subjectivity. Social experience is open to analysis at a level of internal articulation: myths, kinship systems, fashion magazines, consumer objects each constitute a structured world of meaning that derives its intelligibility from its likeness to language. Yet the use of structural linguistics in social theory bears a certain cost: the formalism of linguistics, when carried over into social science, implies a dehistoricization and a weakening of critical powers. Structural linguistics mandates that phenomena be studied synchronically, outside time, and without reference to normative evaluations.

Baudrillard was one of the first thinkers in France to attempt to employ semiology both historically and critically. The thesis of *Consumer Society* was that in advanced capitalism a new structure of meanings had emerged whose effectiveness was based on a logic of differentiation that was subject to analysis only by a semiological theory. "The social logic of consumption," Baudrillard wrote, "is not at all that of the individual appropriation of the use value of goods and services . . . it is not a logic of satisfaction. It is a logic of the production and manipulation of social signifiers."[19] But Marxism missed its analytical boat if it rested with demonstrating that capitalism generated these signifiers to manipulate the masses into unwanted acts of consumption.[20] The point was rather that the signifiers themselves, not the products, had become objects of consumption that drew their power and fascination from being structured into a code. The code, in turn, could be deciphered not by the logic of capital but by the logic of semiology.

Baudrillard's analysis of consumption was thus fully historical because it subordinated semiology to critical theory: the production of commodities had entered a new stage that was accompanied by a new structure of signs, a new linguistic apparatus. Once this new structure of meanings was analyzed semiologically, revealing its structured code, an argument could be developed that radical change must focus on the code, and develop a practice to dismantle it and a strategy to create a new order of symbolic exchange with a new system of signs. Baudrillard's intent was double: to revise semiology so that its formalism and ahistoricity were tamed to the needs of critical theory; and to revise Marxism so that its productivism was tamed to the needs of cultural criticism. The result would be a new critical theory that captured the interdependence of technology and culture, production and symbolic exchange.

The System of Objects and *Consumer Society* carried out these goals by demonstrating the advantages of semiology over the Marxist concept of needs in the analysis of consumerism. If commodities are conceptualized as deriving their value from labor and their use from need, the extraordinary expansion of consumerism since World War II remains a mystery. Why would workers exhaust themselves in labor only to purchase the products that capitalism places on the market, products whose worth may be questioned? According to Marx, human needs are not fixed, but alter with changes in the mode of production. If that is true, capitalism has successfully instituted an infinite cycle of production and consumption. But Marx's analysis overlooked, according to Baudrillard, the function of social exchange. Limited to the metaphor of production in the analysis of social practice, Marx missed the force of the social exchange of meanings that envelops commodities in a non-productivist logic. If, on the other hand, society were seen as a system of symbolic exchange, the power of the code would reveal its force.

Under advanced capitalism, Baudrillard contends, the masses are controlled not only by the need to labor in order to survive but by the need to exchange symbolic differences.[21] Individuals receive their identity in relation to others not primarily from their type of work but from the signs and meanings they display and consume. Taking his cue from Veblen and certain anthropological theories, Baudrillard asserts the importance of commodities as social signifiers, not as material objects. But he avoids the dangers of such theories of emulation by rooting his analysis firmly in the soil of the current social epoch. The shift from the primacy of production to the primacy of exchange has been facilitated by the development of new technologies, such as radio and television. The cultural significance of these technologies is that they emit a single message and constitute a new code: "the message of the consumption of the message."[22] The new media transform the structure of language, of symbolic exchange, creating the conditions in which the new code of consumerism can emerge.

From the vantage point of semiology, the new code is easy enough to decipher. An ad for Pepsi-Cola, for example, pictures a community of all ages, classes, sexes and races enjoying a drink together. The message is clear if subliminal: to drink Pepsi-Cola is not so much to consume a carbonated beverage as to consume a meaning, a sign – that of community.[23] In this ad a value that capitalism destroys (community) is returned to society through the ad. In another example the code operates not as utopian realization but as pressure to conform. Brut cologne is associated with aggressive manhood. Again, to use the product is to consume the meaning – in this case a stereotype of masculinity. The implication of the ad is that those who do not use Brut will not be manly, losing out in the game of sexual conquest.

Although opposite in their strategy, both ads illustrate the mechanism of the code. The product itself is not of primary interest; it must be sold by grafting onto it a set of meanings that have no inherent connection with the product. The set of meanings subject to semiological analysis becomes the dominant aspect of consumption. Unlike Habermas, who sees meanings as scarce in advanced capitalism, Baudrillard discovers a profusion of meanings in the system of consumption. This difference in the two thinkers speaks to the relative value of their sources: the elitist pessimism of the Frankfurt School which, failing to find "authentic" values in mass society, rejects popular and consumer culture out of hand; and the semiology employed by Baudrillard, which grants the validity of popular and consumer culture long enough to carry out a trenchant analysis of it.

In *Pour une critique de l'économie politique du signe* (1972) Baudrillard endeavored to correlate systematically his critical semiology with Marx's critique of political economy. Still remaining within a Marxist framework at least nominally, he tested the general principles of Marx's analysis of the commodity with that of semiology's analysis of the sign. Just as Marx decomposed the commodity into use value and exchange value, so semiology deciphered the sign as signified and signifier. Baudrillard discovered a homology between the sign and the commodity: the signifier is to exchange value what the signified is to use value.[24] The parallelism at the formal level, however, masks a certain misrecognition or ideology which is the effect both of the structuralist concept of the sign and the Marxist notion of the commodity.

The structuralist concept of the sign naturalizes or universalizes what is in fact, according to Baudrillard, a historically based semiological formation. The sign, split off from the referent and intelligible only at the level of the relation of signifier to signifier, is actually a drastic reduction of the symbolic. In a universe of symbols, signifier, signified and referent are integrated in acts of communication. Symbols are characterized by an ambivalence of meaning as they are exchanged from one person to another. The sign, on the contrary, is full, positive, univocal.[25] It is not an inevitable truth about language, but a product of a specific semiological epoch. Programmed by industry and bureaucracy, the sign is part of the strategy of power (*Pour une critique*, p. 91). Removed from the web of mutual reciprocity, the sign is a unilateral message, a communication without a response (p. 138). Signs are made possible by the new technologies of the media in which signifiers flash by potential consumers. Once signifiers have been separated and abstracted in this way, floating free, so to speak, in communicational space, they can be attached to particular commodities by the arbitrary whim of advertisers. Thus a new structure of meaning is instituted that collaborates with the requirements of advanced capitalism.

Marx's concept of the commodity never attains this level of analysis. He neglects the process of transformation by which exchange value becomes a sign (p. 129). Because the conceptual apparatus of Marxism is modeled on production and labor, it cannot make intelligible "the social labor of producing signs" (p. 132), which is based on a different logic. The circulation of signs itself produces surplus value, one based not on profit but on legitimacy (p. 140). At this time, Baudrillard was content to argue that his analysis of the message was parallel to Marx's analysis of the commodity. Just at the point where Marxism became "ideological" because it could not decode the semiology of the commodity, Baudrillard stepped in to enrich and improve upon historical materialism, updating it to the circumstances of advanced capitalism.

Hints of a coming break with Marx were nonetheless present in *Pour une critique*. The point of divergence with Marx centered on the question of the logic of production versus the logic of exchange, the materiality of commodities versus the ideality of the sign. In rejecting the structuralist separation of the sign from the world, Baudrillard argued that the world "is only the effect of the sign" (p. 185). If individuals consumed meanings rather than products, the centerpiece of social theory was symbolic exchange, not the production of goods. Value was created, therefore, not in the labor process but in the communicational structure. In *Pour une critique*, Baudrillard's emphasis was on revising Marx rather than supplanting him, but the seeds of post-Marxist critical theory were already planted.

The break with Marx came only a year later with the publication of *The Mirror of Production*. Here Baudrillard presented in no uncertain terms his critique of Marx's notion of labor, systematically deconstructing the apparatus of the critique of political economy:

> A specter haunts the revolutionary imagination: the phantom of production. Everywhere it sustains an unbridled romanticism of productivity. The critical theory of the *mode* of production does not touch the *principle* of production. All the concepts it articulates describe only the dialectical and historical genealogy of the *contents* of production, leaving production as a *form* intact.[26]

The Marxist concept of labor, Baudrillard proposes, is too close to the liberal notion of *homo economicus* to provide a radical critique of political economy. Like the liberals, Marx reduces practice to labor and society to production. Marx discovered in use value the radical basis for the critique of the liberal notion of exchange value. The labor that goes into the commodity constitutes for Marx its true worth, not the amount for which it is exchanged. The notion of exchange value reduces all labor to one level; it obscures concrete differences between human acts, Marx complains.

Baudrillard responds that to uncover the human essence of labor behind the capitalist shroud of exchange value is not enough. Marxism only "convinces men that they are alienated by the sale of their labor power; hence it censors the much more radical hypothesis that they do not have to be the labor power, the 'unalienable' power of creating value by their labor" (*Mirror*, p. 9). Like liberalism, Marx conceptualized the social field in the mirror of production, presenting back to capitalism its own image, only in an inverted form. A radical critique must rather locate the field that is obscured by liberals and Marxists alike – that of symbolic exchange.

Baudrillard locates the point at which Marxist theory becomes complicit with capitalist productivism by reviewing the stages of the relation of production and exchange presented by Marx in *The Poverty of Philosophy*. During stage one, before capitalism, production was for use by the producers and only the surplus was exchanged. In stage two, that of classical capitalism, all production by industry was exchanged. In stage three, fully developed capitalism, not only industrial production, but everything – "virtue, love, knowledge, consciousness" – is placed on the market for possible exchange (*Mirror*, p. 119). Marx views the spread of capitalist principles beyond the area of production as a "corruption" or a time of "universal venality." For Marx, stage three involves the reflection of the base in the superstructure, a secondary effect of the mode of production. Thus the basic shift for him is from stage one to stage two, stage three being conceived only as the logical working out of the system, its general extension to all social relations.

In his critique Baudrillard wavers not between supplementing Marx and rejecting him but between rejecting him only for the analysis of stage three or rejecting him for the entire genealogy of capitalism. In the weaker critique Baudrillard argues that Marx obscures the significance of the shift to stage three because of his productivist metaphor. Social exchange in stage three, from the semiological perspective outlined above, reveals a structurally new type of domination generated by the code or the sign, a type of domination that cannot be made intelligible through the concept of production. In this case, Marxism becomes inadequate as a critical theory only with the advent of the sign as the general principle of communication. In the stronger critique Baudrillard maintains that the sign and the commodity arose together at the beginning of the process of the birth of capitalism and that the critique of the political economy of the sign is more radical than the critique of political economy from the outset. As a critical category, the mode of signification should perhaps take precedence over the mode of production.

Symbolic Exchange and Death (1976) draws out the pessimistic implications of the theory of the code, marking a change in Baudrillard's political stance.[27] As the politics of the 1960s receded so did Baudrillard's radicalism: from a position of firm leftism he gradually moved to one of bleak fatalism. In *Symbolic Exchange and Death* he searches desperately for a source of radicalism that challenges the absorptive capacities of a system with no fixed determinations, a world where anything can be anything else, where everything is both equivalent to and indifferent to everything else – a society, in short, dominated by the digital logic of the code. Baudrillard's depressing conclusion is that only death escapes the code, only death is an act without an equivalent return, an exchange of values. Death signifies the reversibility of signs in the gift, a truly symbolic act that defies the world of simulacra, models and codes.[28]

Symbolic Exchange and Death is flawed by the totalizing quality of Baudrillard's writing. Still, the value of the book lies in the refinements it provides of many of the themes of Baudrillard's earlier works. In it Baudrillard grapples, as nowhere before, with the problem of characterizing the structure of communication in a world dominated by the media. This important issue, too much neglected by critical theory, becomes the mainstay of his writing after 1976. Although Baudrillard treats this theme with hyperbole and vague formulations, he has initiated a line of thought that is fundamental to a reconstitution of critical theory. While this project is somewhat akin to the recent work of Habermas, Baudrillard wrestles with the communication structure of the media, whereas his German counterpart pursues the quixotic end of defining the "ideal speech situation."[29]

In *On Seduction* (1979) Baudrillard makes a turn toward a poststructuralist critique of the hermeneutics of suspicion. Theories that deny the surface "appearance" of things in favor of a hidden structure or essence, theories such as Marxism, psychoanalysis and structuralism, now come under attack. These interpretive strategies all privilege forms of rationality. Against them Baudrillard celebrates a Nietzschean critique of the "truth" and favors a model based on what he calls "seduction." Seduction plays on the surface, thereby challenging theories that "go beyond" the manifest to the latent. The model of seduction prefigures Baudrillard's later term, the hyper-real, with all of its postmodernist implications. At the close of the book, Baudrillard tentatively suggests that seduction might be a model to replace the model of production.

In *Simulacra and Simulations* (1981) Baudrillard extends, some would say totalizes, his theory of commodity culture. No longer does the code take priority over or even precede the consumer object. The distinctions between object and representation, thing and idea, are no longer valid. In their place Baudrillard fathoms a strange new world constructed out of models of simulacra which have no referent or ground in any "reality" except their own. Simulations are different from fictions or lies in that the former not only present an absence as a presence, the imaginary as the real, they also undermine any contrast to the real, absorbing the real within themselves. Instead of a "real" economy of commodities that is somehow bypassed by an "unreal" myriad of advertising images, Baudrillard now discerns only a hyper-reality, a world of self-referential signs. He has moved from the TV ad, which, however, never completely erases the commodity it solicits, to the TV newscast, which creates the news if only to be able to narrate it, or the soap opera, whose daily events are both referent and reality for many viewers.

If Baudrillard's argument of hyper-reality has a modicum of validity, the position of the New Historicists and Deconstructionists must be taken seriously. The self-referentiality of language, which they promote against materialists, phenomenologists, realists and historicists as the key to textual analysis, now in Baudrillard's hands becomes the first principle of social existence in the era of high-tech capitalism. Critical theory faces the formidable task of unveiling structures of domination when no one is dominating, nothing is being dominated and no ground exists for a principle of liberation from domination. If Auschwitz is the sign of total tyranny as the production of death, the world of "hyper-reality" bypasses the distinction between death and life.[30]

The pessimistic implications of *Simulacra and Simulations* are brought home in *Fatal Strategies*. Here Baudrillard attempts to think the social world from the point of view of the object, a seeming oxymoron. Like the poststructuralists, Baudrillard assumes that the era of the representational subject is past. One can no longer comprehend the world as if the Kantian categories of time, space, causality, etc., are necessary, universal paths to truth. Baudrillard takes this to imply that the subject no longer provides a vantage point on reality. The privileged position has shifted to the object, specifically to the hyper-real object, the simulated object. In place of a logic of the subject, Baudrillard proposes a logic of the object, and this is his "fatal strategy." As the reader will discover, the world unveiled by Baudrillard, the world from within the object, looks remarkably like the world as seen from the position of postmodernists.[31]

Baudrillard is not disputing the trivial issue that reason is operative in some actions, that if I want to arrive at the next block, for example, I can assume a Newtonian universe (common sense), plan a course of action (to walk straight for x meters), carry out the action, and finally fulfill my goal by arriving at the point in question. What is in doubt is that this sort of thinking enables a historically informed grasp of the present in general. According to Baudrillard, it does not. The concurrent spread of the hyper-real through the media and the collapse of liberal and Marxist politics as master narratives deprive the rational subject of its privileged access to truth. In an important sense individuals are no longer citizens, eager to maximize their civil rights, nor proletarians, anticipating the onset of communism. They are rather consumers, and hence the prey of objects as defined by the code. In this sense, only the "fatal strategy" of the point of view of the object provides any understanding of the present situation.

In a more recent essay, "The Masses: The Implosion of the Social in the Media," Baudrillard recapitulates the theme of his work in the 1980s: the media generate a world of simulations which is immune to rationalist critique, be it Marxist or liberal. The media present an excess of information and they do so in a manner that precludes response by the recipient. This simulated reality has no referent, no ground, no source. It operates outside the logic of representation. But the masses have found a way of subverting it: the strategy of silence or passivity.[32] Baudrillard thinks that by absorbing the simulations of the media, by failing to respond, the masses undermine the code.[33] Whatever the value of this position it represents a new way of understanding the impact of the media. Instead of complaining about the alienation of the media or the terrorism of the code, Baudrillard proposes a way out: silence. Critical theorists will certainly not remain silent about Baudrillard's paradoxical revolutionary strategy. In fact, more suggestive approaches to the question of resistance have been offered by Pierre Bourdieu and Michel de Certeau. In *The Practice of Everyday Life*, de Certeau argues that the masses resignify meanings that are presented to them in the media, in consumer objects, in the layout of city streets.[34] De Certeau's position on resistance seems more heuristic and more sensible than Baudrillard's.

III

Baudrillard's writing is open to several criticisms. He fails to define his major terms, such as the code; his writing style is hyperbolic and declarative, often lacking sustained, systematic analysis when it is appropriate; he totalizes his insights, refusing to qualify or delimit his claims. He writes about particular experiences, television images, as if nothing else in society mattered, extrapolating a bleak view of the world from that limited base. He ignores contradictory evidence such as the many benefits afforded by the new media, for example, by promoting progressive movements concerning civil rights and the environment, by providing vital information to the populace (the Vietnam War) and counteracting parochialism with humanizing images of foreigners. The instant, worldwide availability of information has changed human society forever, probably for the good.

Nevertheless Baudrillard's work is an invaluable beginning for the comprehension of the impact of new communication forms on society. He has introduced a language-based analysis of new kinds of social experience, experience that is sure to become increasingly characteristic of advanced societies. His work shatters the existing foundations for critical social theory, showing how the privilege they give to labor and their rationalist epistemologies are inadequate for the analysis of the media and other new social activities. In these regards he joins with Derrida's critique of logocentrism and Foucault's critique of the human sciences. Unlike these poststructuralist thinkers, Baudrillard fails to reflect on the epistemological novelties he introduces, rendering his work open to the charges outlined above. For the critical theorist, Baudrillard represents the beginning of a line of thought, one that is open to development and refinement by others.

The tendency to give priority to symbolic exchanges rather than labor is found in the recent work of both Baudrillard and Habermas.[35] Both have enlarged the scope of critical theory to encompass the phenomenon of language and both have placed technology in a closer relationship with culture than Marx did. The mode of signification becomes as central to critical theory as the mode of production. The ideal speech situation for Habermas and symbolic exchange for Baudrillard become the new bases of revolutionary theory. The problem of transforming the mode of production must share the attention of criticism with the problem of transforming the world of meaning, culture and language. By taking critical theory in this direction both Habermas and Baudrillard provide a ground for incorporating into the revolutionary perspective a locus of radicality outside the workplace. Women, minorities, gays, criminals, all the oppressed subcultures may now take part in the process of social transformation on a footing equal to that of the proletariat. Although neither Baudrillard nor Habermas systematically addresses the question of the relation of these subgroups to the mode of signification, there is the clear implication in their thought that this issue is high on the agenda of critical theory.

Although the similarities in direction of the ideas of Baudrillard and Habermas are striking, there remain fundamental differences between them. These divergences can be clarified by comparing their relationship to the left of the late 1960s. In Germany Habermas became a focus of criticism by the New Left, who saw his notion of a public sphere as insufficiently radical. For his part Habermas viewed the students as bourgeois children protesting paternal authority and sexual repression.[36] The significance of their revolt was that they forced into public attention areas of life that hitherto had remained private. They had successfully broken through the shell of bourgeois ideology, revealing the absence of democracy throughout society. In the advanced societies the main problem, however, was that of technology and its undemocratic character. Here the issue could be resolved only through resort to an ideal speech situation. The problem was one "of setting into motion a politically effective discussion that rationally brings the social potential constituted by technical knowledge and ability into a defined and controlled relation to our practical knowledge and will. . . . Our only hope for the rationalization of the power structure lies in conditions that favor political power for thought developing through dialogue."[37] The issue for Habermas was one of creating an institutional framework for undistorted communication. He posited the need for a new subjective basis for rationality; the ideal speech situation would produce a rational society. While appealing to honored and ancient cultural imperatives, Habermas's prescriptions do not go much beyond the contours of the Enlightenment.

Baudrillard was far more enthusiastic than Habermas about the radicalism of the late 1960s. May 1968 was for him an apocalyptic smashing of the repressive code. Against the monologue of the TV, May 1968 presented a festival of symbolic exchange. The streets and walls of Paris shouted down the abstract murmurs of the sign. A new mode of signification was realized in everyday life, if only briefly.[38] The seemingly unconquerable power of the code dissolved in a volley of chatter from students and workers. The new mode of signification was created not through the dialectical maneuvers of the class struggle but in a simple explosion of expressive communication. Like graffiti, the force of symbolic exchange erupted in the semiological field in a sudden burst of meaning. The events of May 1968 confirmed for Baudrillard the poverty of the Marxist notion of revolution. It shattered in one brilliant display of semiological fireworks the notion of the party with its intellectuals, its theory, its cadre, its careful organization and strategy, its duplication of the bourgeois world that it would supplant. The theory of symbolic exchange in Baudrillard's version thus implies a very different world from that of Habermas. The new mode of signification depends not on a new notion of the subject or a new realization of rationality. It denotes instead a new structure of communication in which signifiers would be generated directly in the course of exchange, connected closely to both signified and referent.

Although Baudrillard's critical semiology permits a deeper analysis of the communication structure of advanced capitalism than that of Habermas and avoids undue reliance on concepts of the subject and rationality, it too misses, finally, a satisfactory resolution of a theory of the relation of technology and culture. The danger in Baudrillard's notion of the code is that it accepts too easily the omnipotence of the semiological structure; it totalizes too quickly the pattern of communication that it reveals. As opposed to Habermas's subjectivism, Baudrillard's analysis errs in the direction of objectivism. In his view, floating signifiers pervade the social space without adequate recognition or theoretical account of the continuous disruptions of it by subjects. Baudrillard convincingly theorizes one side of the question – the emission of the signals – but the reception of the signals remains beyond the ken of his semiology. For reception is also an act and it is one that is discontinuous, at least partially, with emission, especially during the epoch of the sign. Revolt against the sign takes place not only in the exceptional collective outburst, such as that of May 1968. Protest and transgression are repeated daily by women who refuse to douse themselves in seductive perfumes, by gays who overtly display their threatening sexuality, by prisoners who do not accept the discipline of the panopticon, by workers who sabotage the smooth flow of the production line, by everyone who draws a line through or erases or marks over the imperatives of the code.

If critical semiology enables critical theory to make intelligible the domination inherent in the mode of signification, it displaces the locus of revolt, failing to present a theory of subjectivity that would account for the gaps and fissures within the system. When Baudrillard argues that escape from the code is found only in death, when meaning finally is not reincorporated into the nightmare of signs, it becomes plain that his objectivism has led to a retreat to a distant desert. Nonetheless, Habermas and, more especially, Baudrillard have carried critical theory far beyond the boundaries of the mode of production to a more fertile theoretical field in which a resolution of the question of technology and culture can be pursued.

PART II

MEDIAS

7

Politics in the Mode of Information: Spike Lee's *Do the Right Thing*

FETISH . . . *An inanimate object worshipped by savages on account of its supposed inherent magical powers, or as being animated by a spirit* (Oxford English Dictionary)

The conflict that broke out in Los Angeles from April 29th to May 2nd, 1992, is said to be one of the worst civil disorders in the history of the United States. Parallels are striking between the LA events, Spike Lee's prophetic film *Do the Right Thing* and the role of the mode of information in each. In *Do the Right Thing* a black man's portable radio was smashed, provoking his beating to death by police; in Los Angeles in late April a videotape of a beating taken by a resident who caught the action by accident was negated by a jury as evidence of police brutality against African-Americans. In both instances, severe civil unrest ensued. In *Do the Right Thing* one of the foreshadowings of the disaster was Radio Raheem's conflict with a Korean grocer; in Los Angeles a black teenage girl's death at the hands of a Korean grocer served the same end, resulting in the intentional destruction of Korean-owned businesses throughout many areas of the city. Both in Los Angeles and in the film the role of the mode of information was highly ambivalent.

Do the Right Thing was disseminated in movie houses around the world, generating much debate and discussion about the condition of African-American communities; newscasts of the Los Angeles events were similarly distributed and argued. The issues of racism and a politics of resistance to it were at the center of both dialogues. The answer to the question "what is the right thing to do for black

Americans suffering oppressive conditions of life?" appears to have been answered in Los Angeles just a few years after the film's release in 1989.

If Lee's film exemplifies one possible appropriation of the mode of information by African-Americans, the Los Angeles disaster indicates another. First, in their violent response to the King verdict, blacks communicated an interpretation of the videotape of the beating different from that of the jury. Viewed from the outside, the trial indicates that in this instance the juridical system determined that images of police beating a defenseless civilian are appropriate when that civilian is black. Blacks agree that this judgment is the norm of the police and the justice system, except they oppose such police repression. The videotape provided them with firm evidence of what they already knew to be the character of police behavior in their communities; the jury's disregard of it was only the final straw. Second, televised images of the riots were for the news media simply a reporting of the truth. On most stations, however, newscasters' canons of objectivity were easily discharged in a barrage of outright condemnation of the participants with little sensitivity for the black community's sense of injustice and hopelessness. At the same time, the coverage of the riots redounded very nicely to the ratings of the networks as the world was riveted to the screen. For the participants the media served otherwise as information about the locations of police presence or its lack and the areas of activity.

In both instances the polysemy and ambivalence of electronically mediated communication is clearly displayed. The characteristic of the mode of information is not simply to serve as a neutral conduit of data but to reconfigure it and to promote its multiple interpretation. In *Do the Right Thing*, Spike Lee accounted for this level of ambiguity in many ways but certainly by presenting the apparently opposing views of Martin Luther King and Malcolm X at the close of his film. In the Los Angeles events this same complexity of electronically mediated communication was played out in the video of the King beating, its dissemination in the media and in the broadcasts of the events themselves enacted in the streets and transposed on TV in living rooms. Were the events immoral violence or venting of outrage at injustice, riot or rebellion? Coincidentally Spike Lee was himself in Los Angeles on April 30th scheduled to present a talk at my campus (the University of California, Irvine, located fifty miles south of Los Angeles) that night, but was unable to appear due to curfew and the closing of the freeways.[1]

In *The Mode of Information* I argued that information technologies, as inscribed in communication practices, generate effects that are politically multifarious. I showed how these effects must first be understood at the cultural level of subject constitution and only then analyzed for their political import. I looked at three areas of electronically mediated communication: television advertisements in which the subject as a centered identity is called into question; databases in which a multiple of the subject is constituted by information which, in turn, is acted upon by remote computers; and computer writing in which the authorial subject is destabilized. Judgments about the political effects of these changes depend on the interpreter's narrative assumptions: if we assume the modern politics of left/right, the effects of electronic communications would appear one way; if we assume a new politics of postmodern/modern, the effects would be interpreted differently.

In this essay I shall shift gears and look at electronically mediated communication not exclusively from the perspective of subject constitution, but more particularly from that of resistance to it by ethnic minorities – the question, that is, of the appropriation of communicative practice by minority groups in forms different from those it assumes in the dominant culture. The general question of resistance is today a difficult one. The theory of resistance in the traditions of Marxism and liberalism grounds freedom in the figure of a rational autonomous individual or group. This figure has been challenged, to my mind effectively, by poststructuralist theory, setting the agenda for a retheorization of the issue. To this end, I find illuminating the work of Michel de Certeau, who argues that practices of everyday life are often forms of "minority" resistance, inscribing temporalities and symbolizations that recode the dominant culture by a subject who is a stranger or "minority" in a space articulated by instrumental, hegemonic strategies.[2] De Certeau perhaps goes too far in ascribing a resistant value to practices that may simply be different from hegemonic norms. Also of interest to the project of theorizing the mode of information in relation to ethnicity and resistance is Homi Bhabha's work on the colonial subject, which I discuss below. These initiatives as well as others that could be mentioned are, however, only a beginning step in the development of a theory of resistance in the present conjuncture. In this essay I explore the relation of the mode of information to minority resistance, highlighting the ambivalent play of forces and political implication in that relation. To this end I shall present two examples, one in which an aspect of the mode of information aids the dominant group, the other in which it facilitates opposition. The second example raises the question of art in the context of resistance in the era of the mode of information.

The first example illustrates the amplification of instrumentally rational power relations of the dominant culture through the mode of information. At issue is the use of the phonograph in the human sciences and in imperialism. In 1885 the *New York Times*, in an article entitled "The Phonograph in Africa," reported that two aspiring anthropologists conceived a novel use for the phonograph: they planned to take the device to Central Africa, record native languages, and return to disseminate their acquisition among the community of linguists. The newly invented communications technology would thus benefit the knowledge of mankind, participating in the Enlightenment metanarrative of emancipation.

But the *New York Times*'s reporter, equally inventive, imagines a less disinterested application of the phonograph:

> Not only would the native Kings have an unbounded respect for the proprietors of such a wonderful fetich [sic], but they could be induced or entrapped into making remarks in the presence of the phonograph which could afterward be reproduced with excellent effect. For example, no African would venture to disobey the voice of his King ordering him to "bring the white men food", and the fact that the voice issued from the phonograph instead of the King's own lips would add, if anything, additional force to the order.... The travellers could describe the phonograph as a new and improved portable god, and call upon the native Kings to obey it. A god capable of speaking, and even of carrying on a conversation, in the presence of swarms of hearers could be something entirely new in Central Africa, where the local gods are constructed of billets of wood, and are hopelessly dumb. There is not a central African who could dare refuse to obey the phonograph god.[3]

In this journalist's imperialist and instrumentalist imagination, the phonograph translates immediately into its potential for domination. Note the use of the term "fetish" in its liberal, Enlightenment meaning as an object endowed with spiritual powers in a non-Western, "primitive," culture of magic. In this usage the term is demeaning, set in contrast with Western techno-scientific rationality. Fetishism here is a wrongful projection of subjectivity into a world of objects. The journalist presupposes a dualism of subject and object with the subject as agent, set apart from a passive multiplicity of objects which are open to control by rational operations of subjects.

In the journalist's discourse, the story of Western civilization's domination of the globe since the inventions of compasses and guns continues unchanged with the advent of the phonograph. Western science and technology directly magnify Western powers of domination. Non-Western peoples are constructed in this imperialist narrative as credulous children who easily succumb to the superior intelligence of the West. African culture is here no more than a bundle of superstitions that provide no resistance to the exercise of Western rationality. Local gods and their human chiefs cower before the Western mind materially incarnate in instruments of control. The journalist does not imagine a credible African appropriation of the technology with possibly important results for African resistance to white domination and for promoting new techno-cultural combinations with various African cultures.

The phonograph was a forerunner of technologies of electronically mediated communication, of an emerging mode of information that potentially challenges established Western discourses. Communicative practices in the mode of information destabilize the Cartesian subject position – the rationally centered subject that looks upon the world as objects open to its control – and to this extent also has effects upon imperialist discourse in the age of industrial capitalism which is grounded in that position. But the *New York Times* piece exemplifies a certain plasticity of Western discourse, the way it easily incorporates new, possibly disorienting cultural objects such as the phonograph into the established configurations of power. African peoples are, for the *Times* journalist, no more than passive material for white control through new technologies. The phonograph, a technology of information, is for the journalist no different from earlier technologies, such as firearms, that control material objects.

Of course, the *Times* journalist ignored, in racist fashion, the way Africans and African-Americans from the start appropriated Western technologies to their own ends, inventing uses for them in relation to their particular needs. Ironically, the phonograph along with other electronic technologies of music reproduction, provides one of the richest examples of such resistance. Writers on black culture often note the prominence of music itself as a central form of resistance both during and after slavery.[4] And they also point to the creativity of African-Americans in transforming objects from daily life into musi-

cal instruments. Dick Hebdige traces Caribbean steel bands to carni-
val in Trinidad in 1937: "By raiding kitchens and rubbish dumps,
they had collected together a formidable range of buckets, frying
pans, oil drums and dustbin lids to make up the first 'orchestra of
steel.' "[5] From the perspective of this essay, the most important
appropriation came with the phonograph. Black disc jockeys in the
Caribbean kept dancers interested in their music by shouting over the
instruments, a practice that echoes an African form of competitive
calling or boasting. Hebdige traces a line of development in this
adaptation of the phonograph: ". . . to understand the development
of rockers and heavy instrumental dub, we have to go back to the
early days of the sound system recordings. We have seen how djs . . .
used to add spice to the instrumental records they were playing by
shouting out their favourite catchphrases over the microphone. These
talk overs or toasts soon became a popular feature of the blues
dances. After a while, the djs began adding electronic sound effects –
echo and reverb – to make the records sound even more unusual.
Gradually . . . more sophisticated recordings were made, using a
number of different instrumental and vocal tracks."[6] The rap music of
today, which began in New York, derives from these Caribbean
traditions; a dj from Jamaica emigrated to the South Bronx, changing
"talk overs" into their now popular form.[7]

The great variety of African-American adaptations of the technologies of music-making and reproduction are only hinted at in these
developments. More drastic uses of electronic media have a long, rich
history. Hebdige writes: "Some of these musics had been created by
mixing together sounds and rhythms from different sources. When
music from two or more sources is so completely blended that a new
sound is created it is sometimes called *fusion* music. . . . Hip hop is a
good example of this second type of music. In hip hop the hard funk
beat stays the same throughout but the dj mixes in snatches of sound
from other records. A hip hop record can contain recognisable
snatches of hard rock, electro funk, salsa, soul, new wave, jazz, and
so on. In fact a hip hop dj can pull in any sound, from a recording of
a car screeching round a corner or a television news broadcast to
Frank Sinatra singing *My Way*."[8] Thus black music incorporates an
astonishing variety of techniques that make new use of electronic
mediation: talk overs, switching between turntables, "scratching"
(spinning the record back and forth while it turns), tape splicing to
create completely new recording from bits of existing work, and
finally pirate radio stations.

In Britain black owners of sound systems developed a sort of technological performance art that resembles the work of Laurie Anderson. Adding to turntables, amplifiers and speakers, they introduced into the musical recording reverb, synthesized sound, bits from various tape recorders and the MCs lyrics and "chatting."[9] Another person, "the selector," chose the music in response to the mood of the audience and dancers. In some cases multiple groups of sound system performers work at the same time, competing with one another for the audience's approval. "Clash dances" feature two groups who alternate playing and "performing" the music in a kind of toasting competition. The sound system groups are so important a component of British black music that many develop followings, called "posses," groups who follow the band from site to site. These phenomena indicate a drastic adaptation of technologies of music reproduction, a far cry from the "fetishism in hearing" that Adorno complained was a degradation endemic to music on the radio and the phonograph.[10] As Paul Gilroy claims, "Sound system culture redefines the meaning of the term performance by separating the input of the artists who originally made the recording from the equally important work of those who adapt and rework it so that it directly expresses the moment in which it is being consumed, however remote this may be from the original context of production."[11] In this appropriation of technology, electronically mediated communication is fused with traditions of African oral culture to produce a new phenomenon. If they are forms of resistance to the dominant culture, these sound system performances also betray their own difficulties. The MCs and selectors tend to be men, with restricted roles for women, and the events are often marked by the violence that is bred in the oppressive conditions of the black community.[12]

In British black communities of the 1980s, radio piracy was a form of protest against the limited types of music played by the licenced stations. One feature of the mode of information that assisted this development is the low cost of electronic technologies. Hebdige writes: "... the real breakthrough in radio piracy occurred when cheap portable transmitters came on the market. ... All they needed was a good quality cassette recorder, a transmitter and a high roof."[13] With well over 140 stations broadcasting, many to a forty-mile radius of listeners, the British black community resisted the homogenization of music typical of the large stations.[14] And the pirates took full advantage of the black traditions of scratching and mixing and doing so on the air with live broadcasts. This is a far cry from the journalist's proposal of using the phonograph to dupe Africans into submission to Western imperialists.

A further example of the imbrication of the mode of information into the question of politics suggests a somewhat different cultural response. In Spike Lee's film *Do the Right Thing* (1989), one denizen of the street scene is Radio Raheem, a big, imposing youth, mute and sullen, who appears always with his enormous portable stereo blaring rap music at full volume. The figure of Radio Raheem may be taken as Spike Lee's effort to depict the African-American appropriation of one instance of the mode of information. And perhaps Radio Raheem is a synecdoche for the director; Lee's film itself exemplifies that appropriation since film is a type of electronically mediated communication. In addition *Do the Right Thing* has more general significance for the black film community since it played a crucial, pioneering role in the recent wave of black films that have achieved wide distribution.[15] These films (most notably Matty Rich's *Straight out of Brooklyn* and John Singleton's *Boyz N the Hood*, but many others as well), like Lee's, portray black culture and society from various black points of view, in sharp contrast to the mainstream Hollywood depiction. This achievement of course runs the danger of cooptation, both by the film industry interested largely in box-office receipts and with an audience interested in diversions and exoticisms. In sum, Lee's ambivalently successful appropriation of the mode of information in *Do the Right Thing* is itself doubled in the figure of Radio Raheem, lending importance to a character whose significance might otherwise be minimized in the reading of the film.

Lee's movie has been severely criticized by Wahneema Lubiano for its essentializing identity politics, its masculinism, its uncritical celebration of the Puritan work ethic.[16] Yet if we limit our focus to the character of Radio Raheem and the issue of the mode of information, a somewhat different understanding of the film emerges. *Do the Right Thing* portrays the African-American world of Brooklyn in 1989 as a patchwork of conflicts. Black versus white, black versus Korean, black versus Latino, young versus old, male versus female (although the women characters are stereotyped and subordinated to the men),[17] brother versus sister, father versus son, brother versus brother, police versus community, small capitalist versus consumer – the film is an endless series of hostilities, put downs, fights, arguments, skirmishes, and finally murder.[18] Radio Raheem is a privileged figure in this respect as well, since he is the only person in the web of conflicts who is killed. In the context of generalized conflict, Radio

Raheem's death highlights the danger of black resistance by its appro-priation of the mode of information. Many of the other conflicts depicted in the film are not destructive but constructive, serving to bind together a community under stress. At one point in the film, for example, Radio Raheem confronts a Latino neighbor in a duel of boom boxes, Raheem winning the contest. A situation that might have ended in violence between two ethnic minorities is defused and a modus vivendi between the two groups is buttressed. Radio Raheem himself is not as fortunate.

The hostility between blacks and whites in particular is at stake in his character. Raheem and his music machine spark the film's climac-tic racial conflict: Raheem, blaring radio perched on his shoulder, enters Sal's Famous Pizza Parlor. An argument ensues in which the white owner screams an appeal for quiet to Raheem over the din of his music, finally in frustration smashing Raheem's machine. In the end, after the police have been summoned, Raheem too is smashed into silence, destroyed like his machine. This incident echoed an earlier scene in which Sal made the same demand for quiet. At that time Radio Raheem insisted on being asked politely to turn the music down. Sal complied by saying "please" and Radio attenu-ated the volume. The second time, however, Radio was incited by Buggin' Out, who was protesting the exclusive display of photos of Italian Americans in a pizzeria habituated predominantly by Afri-can-Americans. At issue in the photo display is the question of repre-sentation, another synecdoche for Lee's film. Sal's insistence on quieting the music, like the absence of African-Americans in the photo display, is an instance of the white entrepreneur's insensitivity to the black community. The conflict with Radio Raheem is thus overdetermined.

Music is an important motif in this saga of American race rela-tions: the film opens with Mookie's girlfriend, Tina, dancing to Public Enemy's "Fight the Power"; the black characters are introduced waking up to sounds of the local black radio station; the soundtrack generally is rich with rap music. But in the ghetto street scene the music is not "live." Instead it arrives through electronic mediation, through a variety of devices by which the black community affirms its devotion to music, reshaping the technology of other dominant groups, white and Asian, to its own purposes. This reshaping and appropriation, however, is in part resistance to the dominant white culture: the radio station is staffed by blacks and plays only black music; Raheem's radio, always with him, is the catalyst of conflicts between blacks and other groups. Within the black community, Radio Raheem at times irritates those close enough to him to be affected by the music but generally has an accepted place in the network of relations in daily life. Like the three middle-aged men whose conversations punctuate the film, Radio Raheem is one character in a patchwork fabric of African-American street culture. But Radio Raheem is more than an acknowledged member of the community: he is an extension of the radio station; he brings African-American music into the street, disseminating it in the public space of the community. Radio Raheem is thus an image of the African-American community's appropriation of information technology for the political purpose of consolidating community bonds. Yet compared to the variety of technological adaptations, in the case of Radio Raheem and in the case of the radio station, Spike Lee invokes somewhat unimaginative forms of this appropriation: Radio Raheem merely plays pre-recorded cassettes and the radio station dj simply plays commercial recordings, a far cry from the sound system men of London or the rap musicians of Harlem.

Yet the boom box serves Lee well as an icon of racial conflict. Thomas Doherty argues, "As an Ur-symbol of interracial animosity and class style wars, the boom box is a perfect radiator for black anger and white noise (and vice versa) . . . the ghetto blaster is the easiest way for the underclass to exact vengeance and aggression on an unwary bourgeois. In . . . any metropolis with public transportation . . . a black youth strolling onto a subway car with his personal, multidecibel sound track sends up red-alert signals and draws out palpable racial vibes. An urban commonplace, it has become something of a mass-media leitmotif. . . . Lee . . . is the only director capable of shouldering the boom box from the other side of the speakers."[19] Lee deploys a racially loaded cliché, transforming it into a vehicle of expression for a black community.

Radio Raheem speaks only three times in the entire movie. First, wanting to buy batteries for his stereo, he argues with a Korean merchant. Next he engages the main character, Mookie, in a conversation about life. Finally he argues with Sal over the loudness of his stereo. Only on the second occasion, the only one not concerned directly with his stereo, does Radio Raheem express a point of view, one that both is replete with Manichean madness and strikes at the heart of the film's position on white/black relations. Significantly, this speech occurs immediately before the scene in Sal's pizzeria which ends in Radio Raheem's death at the hands of the police, and it prefigures that outcome. It also echoes Robert Mitchum in *Night of the Hunter*.

> *Radio Raheem (to Mookie):*
> Let me tell you the story of Right-Hand-
> Left-Hand – the tale of Good
> and Evil

> *Mookie:*
> I'm listening.

> *Radio Raheem:*
> HATE!

He thrusts up his left hand.

> *Radio Raheem:*
> It was with this hand that Brother
> Cain iced his brother. LOVE!

He thrusts up his right hand.

> *Radio Raheem:*
> See these fingers, they lead straight
> to the soul of man. The right hand.
> The hand of LOVE!

Mookie is buggin'.

> *Radio Raheem:*
> The story of Life is this . . .

He locks his hands and writhes, cracking the joints.

> *Radio Raheem:*
> STATIC! One hand is always
> fighting the other. Left Hand Hate
> is kicking much ass and it looks
> like Right Hand Love is finished.
> Hold up. Stop the presses! Love
> is coming back, yes, it's Love.
> Love has won. Left Hand Hate
> KO'ed by Love.

Mookie doesn't know what to say, so he doesn't say anything.

> *Radio Raheem:*
> Brother Mookie, if I love you I
> love you, but if I hate you . . .
>
> *Mookie:*
> I understand.
>
> *Radio Raheem:*
> I love you, my brother.
>
> *Mookie:*
> I love you, Black.[20]

Life for Radio Raheem is a struggle between Love and Hate, an opposition that also characterizes the epigrams from Martin Luther King and Malcolm X which appear at the conclusion of the film, framing it with two opposite statements of "what is to be done": protest non-violently against racism (loving the oppressive brother) or struggling violently, if defensively, against it. Lee's film intentionally does not prescribe which is the right thing to do, presenting both as the condition of the African-American community. But menacing Radio Raheem, just before he is killed by the police, decides for love, at least among blacks. And Mookie, who is confused by Radio Raheem's cryptic logic, understands the gist of his message of love. Yet Radio Raheem is hardly a saint of love. In the script, Lee characterizes him as a "victim of materialism and a misplaced sense of values," a person who depends on a material object as "the one thing that gave him any sense of worth"[21] – in short, a fetishist. Radio Raheem is the emblem of black youth who are destroyed by white society, even to the extent that the only good in their lives (the stereo) comes from that other, oppressive world. At this level the stereo stands for the drugs that are noticeably absent from the film, the narcotic of fetishistic consumption that pacifies a people who lead lives of misery and oppression.

Raheem's radio, as an image and a point of enunciation, serves also as an ambivalent fetish. The boom box stereotypes him (and is a type of stereo) for the white audience and simultaneously, for the black audience, it is a synecdochic sign of protest against white domination. In white, racist discourse, the boom box is a visual and sonic index of the black underclass. Blacks in this white discourse are those who carry boom boxes – those who idly listen to music, who rudely invade with loud noise the space of those around them, who defy both law and civility by turning the obtrusive boom box on in buses and other inappropriate, even illegal public places. The boom box is thus one of the icons that fixes black identity in white discourse as the position of the other, as those who will never be white and who are permanently inferior. It establishes racial stereotype as a stable essence both affirming and disavowing difference.

In psychoanalysis fetishes emerge in the play of desire as displaced objects of repressed gender difference. The anxiety aroused by the recognition of difference is deflected onto a fetish while it is simultaneously disavowed. The fetish protects the stability of the subject's (sexual) identity while conserving the fact of difference. Applying the psychoanalytic concept of fetishism to the context of postcolonial subject positionality, Homi Bhabha argues that fetishes produce a similar play of signification in regard to racial difference.[22] The fetish is the structural place where the difference of skin color is both denied and affirmed. In the case of the boom box, the fetish arouses in the white racist a combination of anxiety and disgust: it confirms the inferiority of blacks, stabilizing white identity, but also threatens the white with a loss of identity, with a fall into the sonic space of the (black) music. In this case the image/subject position of electronically mediated communication (Radio Raheem) is registered in the political play of the binary opposition white culture/black culture. Lee resorts to an emblem of the mode of information to signify the fetish function of the simultaneous denial and assertion of racial difference.

If we recall the first example of the phonograph, the blare of the blaster is in a sense, for many in the white audience, a return of the voice not of the chief but of the tribe. It resonates with all those imperialist films in which African drums pound out the force of the natives in their (futile) effort to combat the intrusion of colonial invaders. To the extent that Radio Raheem recalls that aural gesture, he provides closure for the racist viewer, defining blacks as a strange other, an enemy that must be contained or destroyed. The sounds that emanate from him reproduce the otherness of Africa as a threat that must be quashed.

In yet another meaning of the term fetish, as a commodity fetish in Marx's sense,[23] the boom box signifies the integration of blacks into consumer culture. African-Americans participate in the dominant culture by purchasing objects for the enhancement of their daily life. They consume fetishes and misrecognize the labor value of the commodity, a misrecognition that depoliticizes the economic structure. The worker/producer becomes hidden before the glitter of the commodity fetish, as the true structure of capitalism is occluded and hence removed from the class struggle. But this participation in consumer culture is not a complete assimilation of a minority by the hegemonic majority. Blacks adapt the blaster to deploy their (musical) culture, the film indicates, so as to invade the space of the whites, to contest the pacification of the black community. Here the mechanism of the psychoanalytic fetish operates for the blacks as a way both to deny racial difference (blacks use high tech cultural objects just as whites do) and to maintain that difference (blacks play the machine at high volumes and they do so with their own music). The fetish once again affirms and negates difference. In terms of Appadurai's concept of global culture, in which objects are marked and remarked as they move from one ethnic context to another, the portable stereo as commodity, originating in Japanese culture, where intrusion into the space of others is highly frowned upon, is transformed in the black ghetto, taking on the markings of a different cultural system.[24]

The character Raheem illustrates an important theme in the mode of information: the way electronically mediated communication constitutes new forms of subjectivity. In the film, the black community calls him "Radio Raheem," acknowledging the symbiosis of man and machine in his personage. As mute as Raheem is, so loud is Radio. United in one subject position Radio Raheem is represented as a black version of an android-like RoboCop with the radio always near his body, on his back or held in front of him. In this case his identity unites, in one body image, high technology with subordinate marginality, appropriating the dominant culture for its own enjoyment (of music) while exuding anger against domination by extreme amplification. Raheem is so fused with Radio that when the latter is smashed by Sal, the rage of the former, denied its usual channel of expression, bursts forth in furious violence against the white man, destroying what it can around it only finally to succumb to the white man's superior force of numbers and arms. This black android, unlike his white counterpart, RoboCop, is not an instrument of violence against evil: instead he represents the community in the street, the living bond that unites African-Americans through their music, however mediated by Japanese-Western technology. Through Radio Raheem the pulses of the black people insistently resonate in open space, a continuous affirmation of that culture.

bell hooks suggests that Raheem's death may evoke no sympathy from most white audiences.[25] If this is true, I suggest it may be due to Raheem's manner of appropriating media technology in a figure that refutes the rational autonomous subject of white male society.[26] Raheem's appropriation of technology (from portable stereo to boom box) distances him from middle-class white culture and white audiences. If the Raheem figure cannot evoke identification from racist white audiences, as bell hooks bemoans, it is precisely because of this cultural difference. In *Do the Right Thing*, Spike Lee affirms that difference and shows how it must unfold and end (in Raheem's death), given the balance of forces in the present conjuncture. The film also pluralizes and complicates race relations by treating conflicts between Latinos, Asians and African-Americans, indicating that the anxiety of racism is not limited to black/white confrontations. (But this aspect of the film leads beyond the discussion of the relation of the film to the mode of information.) Raheem's death represents the impossibility, in the present array of social forces, of a secure black appropriation of the mode of information, an indication of the political work that remains to be done, if the right thing is done, in order for blacks to upset the mechanisms of domination that confront them and create subject positions for themselves that modulate the current technology to their own sounds.

From the early discourse on the application of the phonograph in white culture to a recent appropriation of the portable stereo in a representation of the black ghetto, the context of electronically mediated communication has changed the situation. In the late nineteenth-century example, the journalist complacently disregarded the possibility of an African appropriation of the phonograph into their cultural practice, or an application of it in anti-colonial struggles. In the late twentieth century, minority social groups in the United States are in a different position, and are confronted, even colonized, by a new array of instruments of electronic mediation. Spike Lee's film, with his representation of Radio Raheem [is Raheem a double for Lee himself, a figure who carries a black appropriation of white cinema, another form of electronically mediated communication, defiantly into that group's space?], is a black invention within the dominant white world. One of the attributes of some aspects of the mode of information in the present is its relative ease of dissemination, its quality of availability for use by minority cultures. In general, technologies like television and the computer enable communication at a distance, tending to isolate individuals from their community. Uniquely, the portable stereo in the black street scene is part of a minority public culture, not distancing the individual from the group but amplifying the group's ethos (its music in this case) in public space.

This is not to say that the congerie of electronically mediated communications works in a linear manner to strengthen the position of the Other of white society. The mode of information is potentially a source of both domination and liberation. As each of its constructs are inserted into various cultural spaces, their specific political effects are unpredictable and depend on the particular relation of forces in each context. But they are important objects of struggle and contestation whose final signification remains in doubt.

In *The Mode of Information* I argue that electronically mediated communication destabilizes the autonomous subject of Western culture and society by multiplying, fracturing and dispersing it. In *Do the Right Thing* Spike Lee's ambiguous character Radio Raheem, defiant victim and mute belligerent, constitutes subjectivity through electronically mediated technology, one which does not fit within that dynamic. Lee seems to suggest that, in African-American working-class communities, information technologies are appropriated/imposed and constitute subjects differently from the way the mechanism operates in the dominant white culture. Like Lee, the black filmmaker, Radio Raheem acknowledges by use the power of the other's technology but also transforms it by his own cultural designs. Unlike others in the community who also appropriate these technologies, Radio Raheem constitutes his identity in this appropriation, radicalizing its impact upon himself. And yet for Lee, Radio Raheem is the catalyst of strife between white and black and its victim as well. The appropriation of the other's technology is, for Lee, dangerous and may itself become the terrain of conflict.

The resistant subject position suggested by Radio Raheem, following a trajectory not in relation to the Cartesian subject but in relation to that of an Other, elicits a reconceptualization of the term "fetish." For if the radio fetish is a mystified commodity, as Spike Lee claims, it also has a more positive determination: it provides a focal point for the inscription of alternative subject positions. In *Feminizing the Fetish*, Emily Apter offers just such a revision. She indicates how objects of esteem in African culture are labelled fetishes by whites, but that these same objects, once removed from Africa and installed in European museums, become "fetishes" *for* Western culture, although without allowing the use of the term. The fetish object thus bears a complex movement of exchanges between cultures that disrupts a dismissive use of the term fetish. Apter also shows how the fetish was a central problem for psychiatry in the nineteenth century, the crux of the problem of defining normal sexuality. Since fetishes are harmless pleasures but ones clearly divergent from a sexuality that would be limited to genital, reproductive practices, it had to be given a negative valorization.[27] In these historical conjunctures, desire was contained by the occlusion of the fetish. Perhaps the character of Radio Raheem indicates another path of fetishization, a path of over-investment in the object of electronic mediation as a lever to open spaces of resistant subject positions, to explore counter-cathexes, ones not legitimized by the dominant culture. As Gilroy says, "Culture is not a fixed and impermeable feature of social relations. Its forms change, develop, combine and are dispersed in historical processes. The syncretic cultures of black Britain . . . have been able to detach cultural practices from their origins and use them to found and extend the new patterns of metacommunication which give their community substance and collective identity."[28]

Do the Right Thing might then be interpreted as an exploration of African-American identity formation under the difficult conditions of poverty and subordination and within the ambiguous circumstances of the mode of information. As Olaniyan points out, Lee avoids essentialism – racial stereotypes, stable identities – by presenting the community as a tapestry of conflicts, united only at the end of the film in the protest against Radio Raheem's death.[29] His cinematic techniques of low-angle shots, saturated colors, juxtaposed vignettes rather than classic narrative structure construct a representation of subjects neither as ideologically hegemonic fixed personas who overcome crises of circumstance nor as exotic others in one-dimensional caricature, but, like Radio Raheem, as contingent articulations, continuously reconfigured in historical conjuncture. In this sense *Do the Right Thing* comes to terms with the postmodern instability of subject position characteristic of the mode of information. Ernesto Laclau writes: "We live in societies in which we are increasingly less able to refer to a single or primary level as the one on which the basic identity of the social agents is constituted. This means, on the one hand, that social agents are becoming more and more 'multiple selves,' with loosely integrated and unstable identities, and on the other, that there is a proliferation of the points in society from which decisions affecting their lives will be taken. As a result, the need to 'fill the gaps' is no longer a 'supplement' to be added to a basic area of constitution of the identity of the agent but instead becomes a *primary* terrain."[30] In Lee's film, Raheem and his radio portray the dynamics of such a conjuncture with the travail of its new configurations of domination.

8

RoboBody

Critical social theory can no longer content itself with the vantage point of the mode of production.[1] Too many things have changed, too many projects have gone awry, too many novelties have been introduced in the means of production, in the relations of production, in the interplay of base and superstructure, in the elements of the superstructure. Theoretical advances in linguistics, structuralism, semiology, poststructuralism, psychoanalytic object relations theory, feminism and communication theory all take their point of departure outside the concept of the mode of production and find their fruitful developments beyond its perimeters. In this theoretical conjuncture I introduce the concept of the mode of information[2] to designate a non-homogeneous cluster of electronically mediated communications. Specifically TV ads, databases and computer[3] writing are symbolic patterns, communications if you will, that require linguistically based theories to explore their operations, their manners of articulation, the forms of domination they incur and the prospects they offer for the project of emancipation.

These elements of the mode of information constitute the subject in new ways. The subject as an agent of history in the form of the liberal autonomous individual or the socialist class conscious collective, the subject as a rational, centered, unified point of perspective opposed to a world of objects that is open to its domination, the subject of male Western culture during the past two centuries is being destabilized, threatened and subverted by new communicational patterns. Quite apart from structural changes in the economy and in politics, quite apart from such "marginal" political movements as those of feminists, ecologists, gay and lesbian activists and anti-nuclear advocates, the familiar cultural practices that accompanied the rise of industrial capitalism arc rapidly disintegrating in the face of the mode of information. Critical theory's sense of the real and the imaginary, the subject and the object, the ideal and the material, inside and outside, male and female, mind and body are all open to fluid transformations, the patterns of which are difficult to discern.

The body is always already culturally inscribed, never a natural object available without mediation for a rational subject (of science). The complication of this poststructuralist position I want to introduce is that industrial society and now postindustrial society, the mode of production and now the mode of information, have inserted in the social space analogues of the human body in the form of increasingly complex tools. Tool-making man makes tools that imitate his own functions. A point has arrived in this process of the machine reproduction of the body when it is the brain that is being reproduced, part by part, in computers and in electronically mediated communication systems in general. An intelligent robot is now a dream of many in the industrial, scientific and university communities. As the functions of the brain are progressively added to the robot, the social world progressively includes a new species of android, one that confronts human beings in a specular relation that deconstructionists tell us is figured as a *mise en abyme*, a perpetual, infinite mirroring.

Verhoeven, the Dutch director of *RoboCop*, presents a postmodern film[4] that situates itself in the mode of information. Seemingly a film in the cops-and-robbers genre, *RoboCop* undermines this presentation by extreme stylization and self-conscious references to other Hollywood productions and more especially to TV serials. Indeed the film opens with a TV newscast so that the movie viewer is repositioned in his or her home watching TV. The action in the film is set against repeated glimpses of people watching television. Everyone in the film – the bad guys, the cops, the idealized victims – watches the same inane game show in which a woman's body is repeatedly displayed and violated by a cake which is thrown not on her face but on her breasts. Murphy (later RoboCop) wears his gun cowboy style, in a compartment on the side of his upper leg. When he "goes for his gun" he always twirls it before aiming. When asked why he does this, Murphy admits that he wants to impress his son who has seen it done by a TV hero, T. J. Laser, and that "I get a kick out of it." His gait resembles an exaggerated John-Wayne swagger. The mandatory violence in the film, while explicit enough to have summoned the censor's scissors, is exaggerated and funny rather than frightening. Japanese monster films are cited in the battle between RoboCop and his nemesis Ed (Enforcement Droid) 209, the creation of Dick Jones, the film's villain. RoboCop is able to elude and finally defeat Ed 209 not through superior strength but through a flaw in Ed's body: he cannot walk downstairs.

The film continuously undermines itself as a film in order to be taken as a TV serial, in order to have its effect at the level of the banal and everyday, in order to reference itself in relation to the viewer's body situated in the intimacy and familiarity of the home.

The film opens with a TV news broadcast in which life is depicted as dangerous and threatening, with imminent risk of nuclear war and social disorder. But a commercial promises to solve the problem of the individual, offering a new model replacement heart that will end all worry. The viewer is introduced to the film through two commonplace discourses which are interconnected: newscasts figure the body as in danger and TV ads promise to overcome all threats to it. This double effect is typical of the discursive practice of television, indeed of all discursive practice: the individual is subject to an imposition of power over the body, which is then, in a second maneuver, said to be resolved. In the case of psychoanalysis, the child is first positioned within the Oedipus complex and then, through the discourse of therapy, offered a resolution. In *RoboCop*, the audience is invited into the discursive game by the familiarity of the introduction: the newscast is like that watched earlier in the evening, before going to the movie. But the commercial, which is part of the verisimilitude of the newscast, is just parodic enough to provide a distancing effect that subverts the play of power over the body.

At issue in the newscast is indeed the body, in this case that of a recently slain Detroit police officer, the news of which the anchorman is providing. In a related story, he announces that Omni Consumer Products, Inc., has contracted to take over the Detroit police department. The story of the officer's death is the reverse image of the main story of the newscast. The structure of the newscast is nuclear war threat (social chaos) + ad for replacement heart (individual salvation). The structure of the Detroit story is policeman killed by criminals (individual death) + capitalist takeover of the police (social salvation). The common theme in this inverse double discourse is the power of technological capitalism over the body: over the social body of Detroit (Omni Consumer Products) and over the individual body (the replacement heart manufacturer).

As the movie develops, it becomes clear that such control over the body is only possible for capitalism through advanced science/technology. Capitalism (OCP) will outperform the state (DPD) only because of its ability to exploit scientific knowledge. The crime problem is defined as the need for a 24-hour cop, one who doesn't eat or sleep, but works relentlessly against crime. The solution to the problem is RoboCop, an android[5] created from a near-dead officer, Murphy. Advanced technology reworks Murphy into the final crimebuster. Science remodels the human body to suit the needs of capitalism, which of course in turn serves to benefit humanity. When the doctors proudly announce they have saved one of Murphy's arms, the project director angrily tells them to "lose it"; he wants "total body prosthesis" for RoboCop. The surgery on the arm is allowed since Murphy is legally dead and anything can be done to him. In the gap between the dead and the living, the android will be born.

The change from the mode of production to the mode of information is directly reflected in *RoboCop*. The important scenes are two meetings of the board of directors of OCP, the sensitive hub of capitalism. In both cases the themes are violence, capitalism and the body, and in each case the issue is decided not by brute force but by information technologies. This is evident in the first scene. Significantly, the first violence in the film results from a problem of information: Ed is being demonstrated at a board meeting of Omni Consumer Products corporation. It is programmed to destroy anyone who draws a gun on it. When one of the executives does so to demonstrate Ed's efficient power, a "glitch" is revealed in Ed's design. The executive is told to "put down your weapon" but Ed doesn't hear the response and "blows him away."

At the concluding board of directors' meeting, after being unable to arrest the bad guy, Dick Jones, RoboCop replays his memory-tape, providing evidence of Jones's conspiracy to murder, and thereby evading the limitations of his programmed instructions and defeating his protagonist. When the brute force of his mechanism has been stifled by a computer "program," highly classified directive 4, that inhibits him from arresting his own superiors, another informational system nullifies the limit of his programming – he has been supplied with visual and aural memory in tape format. In the mode of information, decisive powers are not mechanical but informational.

Verhoeven gives us a representation of a new field of forces: in the background of the film are capitalism with its relentless search for profits and Hollywood escapist violence (cops and robbers, monsters, good and evil). But something new is added that at one level reinforces these themes and at another level undermines them. New discursive practices of the mode of information now take the lead in controlling and empowering the body: science reconfigures the body at will and electronically mediated communication (taped memory) works to undo the forces of evil. The mode of information overlays the traditional themes of capitalism and Hollywood film genres. The outcome of the drama rests with the question of who will best manipulate the capabilities of the mode of information – the bad guys (Dick Jones et al.) or the good guys (Murphy and Lewis, his woman partner).

The sacchrymose ending of the film, in which capitalism, romance and morality are aligned and victorious, is partially undermined in two ways: (1) as in a "Starsky and Hutch" segment, the happy ending is so predictable that it cannot be taken seriously; and (2) the political impact of the film is to expose the bizarre repositioning of the body in the mode of information. Still, the film is presented in the institutional framework of the "culture industry" and as such its purpose is to make a profit and divert its audience from attending critically to structures of domination that diminish their lives. *RoboCop* differs from more conventional films in its genre by subverting as it reproduces and celebrates the banalities of everyday life in the mode of information.

But Verhoeven has represented one possible line of development of the body in the mode of information. As Baudrillard writes, with the contemporary media, "the dramatic interiority of the subject" has given way. "We are here at the controls of a micro-satellite, in orbit, living no longer as an actor or dramaturge but as a terminal of multiple networks. Television is still the most direct prefiguration of this. . . . This is the time of miniaturization, telecommand and the microprocession of time, bodies, pleasures. . . . This change from human scale to a system of nuclear matrices is visible everywhere: this body, our body, often appears simply superfluous, basically useless in its extension, in the multiplicity and complexity of its organs, its tissues and functions, since today everything is concentrated in the brain and in genetic codes."[6] A posthumanist discourse is called for to map the new domains of the body in its new configurations with technology.

9

What Does Wotan Want?
Ambivalent Feminism in
Wagner's *Ring*

In the four operas of the *Ring* cycle, Wagner presents a world, a world in crisis and undergoing change, but a coherent, rule-governed world nonetheless. Using as his raw material the medieval saga of the *Nibelungenlied*,[1] Wagner worked up a presentation of a world in which the central character, Wotan, ruler of this world, attempts to carry out a plan and is unsuccessful in doing so. Such a bare representation of the drama of the *Ring* is highly misleading because everything about Wotan is problematic: his statement of his plan, his will to carry out the statement, his action in relation to the statement, and his relationships to the other characters concerning the statement. In this essay I want to suggest that, in the character of Wotan, Wagner's work explores the limits of a modern, patriarchal subject, and begins to move toward what has emerged as a feminist position. And if this is the case, the criticism of Wagner's work by his friend and later enemy Friedrich Nietzsche loses some of its force and needs to be re-examined.

In this reading I will limit myself to the Porter translation of the text, with some corrections, and to the Boulez/Chereau production,[2] which was televised and therefore widely available. I am not competent in music theory so I will restrict myself to literary, historical and philosophical strategies of analysis.[3] As Samuel Weber insisted in an essay on a different production of the *Ring*, Wagner did write music *drama*, so that a literary analysis, while in some sense not ideal, is certainly permissible and may be fruitful. He goes so far as to argue that "the structural problems of the *Ring* may well be more accessible through a reading that begins with the text rather than with a musical score that often conceals the subtleties of its organization behind a deceptive simplicity."[4] In addition, Philippe Lacoue-Labarthe has shown how the question of the literary is very much at stake in Wagner's music.[5] While not without their problems, non-musical interpretations of Wagner's work may be heuristic and compelling.

Wagner first positions Wotan such that he is able to control the world. In that sense he may be said to represent men in general, or at least men to the degree that they have governed human society. Wotan, King of the Gods, bears every stamp of a European monarch: his virtues and social traits are aristocratic.[6] His marriage to Frika, for example, is a political alliance, and, like all aristocratic marriages, not a sentimental choice but an act which solidifies Wotan's political position. Further, Wotan rules in the manner of feudal kings through a combination of wars and alliances, with the resulting treaties inscribed on his spear, his symbol of office. As Lord of the Earth, Wotan's desire is tantamount to actuality. Yet things are not that simple in the *Ring*.

Alberich, leader of the Nibelungen horde, is nominally Wotan's mortal enemy. A good part of the *Ring* concerns the long struggle between them. Yet Alberich is a would-be ruler of the world and there is much in the text to suggest that, at least in part, he is to be understood as another side of Wotan, a binary opposite whose opposition reveals a likeness more than a difference. Wotan is referred to as "white Alberich" as distinct from the Nibelung, the "black Alberich." In this sense they are two sides of the same coin, brothers, even twin images of each other: each is a man attempting to control the world; each has a male heir who plays a crucial role in this design. Yet as George Bernard Shaw rightly points out, Wotan's ruling strategy is aristocratic while Alberich's modus operandi is capitalist. Alberich pursues power through money which is attained by exploiting the skills and labor of others.[7] What the British socialist does not see, however, is that Wotan and Alberich are not only points of opposition in the class struggle but also comrades in preserving patriarchy. In that sense, Wotan and Alberich are one character: the futility of Alberich's designs may be added to the difficulties of Wotan in a sum that portrays not so much the class struggle but the impasse of the male subject and the impossibility of his modernist project.

By asking "What Does Wotan Want?" I am of course echoing the question of Freud, and perhaps men in general: "What does a woman want?"[8] This question, with its bemused, condescending tone, is normally uttered not as a question but as an answer. It implies that no one knows what women want, not even women. As a "rhetorical" question, it is not meant to be answered. The enunciation of the question ends the discussion, with the masculine position having the last word. Yet of course Freud spent his life answering this question, exploring, mostly with women, the labyrinthine paths of desire. In this sense, Freud's question, far from a rhetorical ploy in the battle of the sexes, is a most serious query, among the most serious interrogatives Freud ever posed. By placing the question "What does a woman want?" where it is in the essay on femininity, Freud belittles his text, providing an alibi in advance for any flaws in his argument. After all, how could someone be blamed if he really could not answer a question that is basically unanswerable? In yet another sense, however, the posing of the question returns power to the position of men: the scientist does provide an answer to the question; logocentrism and the position of the male subject is confirmed because an answer is given: women want a penis. Women, as other, are unbearable and inscrutable to reason; they become comprehensible only to the extent that they desire a man and are only definable to the extent that they are not masculine, that they do not have a penis.

In the *Ring*, Wagner's inability to define a coherent desire or thought for his character Wotan is, I contend, an indication that the modernist social project in its masculine forms is crumbling and that Wagner's problem with Wotan's will emerges as a strength of his text, a sign of his rigorous effort to work through the question of modernity in its philosophical and social forms.[9] In a similar vein, Nietzsche, as Derrida contends,[10] attacked Western philosophy from the position of the woman/other ("supposing truth were a woman") and therefore placed his own work on the side of the other. But at least in his writings on Wagner, Nietzsche was incapable of sustaining a position of feminist critique, of identifying with the maternal other in his battle with philosophical fathers. Instead of explicitly rejecting the misogyny, as he does for example in the case of anti-Semitism, his texts are strewn with essentializing, abusive statements about women. By contrast, negative images of women in the *Ring* – the conventionality of Frika, the cruel seductions of Alberich by the Rhinemaidens – belittle particular qualities of some women in the patriarchal culture of Europe. They avoid the abusive scapegoating strategies that mar Nietzsche's texts and betray his inability to come to grips with his own resentment toward women.

Nietzsche wrote about Wagner from the beginning to the end of his career. His first book, *The Birth of Tragedy* (1871), depicts Wagner as a hero of Dionysus. His last book was *Nietzsche Contra Wagner* (1889), a revised compilation of earlier fragments on the composer. The major piece on Wagner is *The Case of Wagner* (1888). A full discussion of the complex relation of the two men and of their writings on each other is out of place in this short chapter. But a discussion of Nietzsche's interpretation of the *Ring* usefully accents the larger issues of this essay.

Nietzsche posits the theme of redemption as the center of all of Wagner's operas.[11] Thereby the *Ring* falls under the category of slave morality, "decadent" and life-denying, a sickness of the body – in particular the nerves. And this moral configuration Nietzsche associates with the feminine. By contrast the music of Bizet and Mozart are free of Wagnerian "illness." Here there are rhythms and melodies of a high musical order, unlike Wagner's infinite unfolding of leitmotif. Nietzsche goes on repeatedly to accuse Wagner's music and Wagner himself of the moral crime of seduction: "Wagner is a seducer on a large scale"[12] and the like echo over and over in the short essay. For Nietzsche, Wagner's music is part, a good part, of the cultural crisis of Europe, the continuing descent of European man into the hell of slave morality.

At the conclusion of the first postscript to the essay an extraordinary passage links women and Wagner in a vituperative denunciation and at the same time suggests, on the part of Nietzsche, resentment at Wagner's success in relations with women. Nietzsche writes:

Wagner is bad for youths; he is calamitous for women. What is a female Wagnerian, medically speaking? – It seems to me, a doctor can't confront young women too seriously with this alternative for the conscience: one or the other. – But they have already made their choice. One cannot serve two masters when the name of one is Wagner. Wagner has redeemed woman; in return, woman has built Bayreuth for him. All sacrifice, all devotion: one has nothing that one would not give to him. Woman impoverishes herself for the benefit of the master, she becomes touching, she stands naked before him. – The female Wagnerian – the most charming ambiguity that exists today; she *embodies* the cause of Wagner – in her sign his cause triumphs. – Ah, this old robber! He robs our youths, he even robs our women and drags them into his den. – Ah, this old Minotaur! The price we have had to pay for him! Every year trains of the most beautiful maidens and youths are led into his labyrinth, so that he may devour them . . .[13]

This passage smacks of *Moses and Monotheism* and *Totem and Taboo*; it exudes an Oedipal rebellion against a Mosaic father who hordes the beautiful young women, charms them so that they trumpet his cause, sacrifice all for him, go willingly into his den. Thus Nietzsche displays an ambivalence toward women, both desiring them and resenting those, like Wagner, who succeed in winning their favor.

Nietzsche identifies Wagner's music with his success with women.[14] And Wagner's music, Nietzsche is compelled to admit, is feminist: "his main enterprise aims *to emancipate women...*"[15] Wagner presents Brünnhilde as, Nietzsche writes, "the free spirit and immoralist," which are Nietzsche's own terms for *the Übermensch*, for Zarathustra, for all that Nietzsche admired and hoped for. Nietzsche devoted his life to promoting a vision of a new "man" to redeem Europe; Wagner has the effrontery to present a woman as the redeemer. Therefore in Nietzsche's eyes Wagner is a decadent, a nay-sayer of the highest, most dangerous order. Only a full study of this question would do justice to the complexity of the issues at stake. But these brief remarks suggest that Nietzsche's denigrating interpretation of the *Ring* confirms the thematic of this essay, however opposite is his valence from mine. The extent to which Wagner depicts the collapse of the masculine ego and affirms a feminist subject position may now be clarified.

Wotan sings several versions of his plan to maintain power. Wotan's very first words in *Rheingold* plainly aver his intention. Referring to Valhalla, he says, "The sacred hall of the gods is guarded by gate and door: manhood's honor (*Mannes Ehre*), unending power (*ewige Macht*), rise now to endless renown!" and, after Frika's debunking reply, he continues, "Completed, the eternal work! On mountain summits the gods will rule! Proudly rise those glittering walls which in dreams I designed, which my will brought to life. Strong and lordly see it shine; holy, glorious abode!"[16] The honor of *men* is at stake, honor defined by their power which, though represented by the castle, is ultimately a question of "dreams" and "will," a question in short of the subject. Wotan's will is clear: eternal power is what he wants. But if Freud's women do not know what they want, neither do Wagner's men. No sooner has Wotan defined his will, presented it as a closure, than he must revise it, expand it to incorporate something it lacks. Told about the power of the Ring, Wotan insists, "The ring – I must have it!"[17] The closure is opened again; Valhalla does not encompass all power; Wotan's will is a lack. *Rheingold* ends with a cryptic statement by Wotan that the meaning of Valhalla has not completely been revealed, that his full desire remains to be presented: "When all that I've dreamed and planned comes to pass, when victory is mine, you'll understand that name!"[18]

In *The Valkyrie*, Wotan's will is further revealed and complicated. He is threatened by the possibility that Alberich will get the ring from Fafner, but the treaty system that he dominates also restrains him. Only "a man, a hero . . . free of soul . . . who acts alone, by his own design – that man can do what the god must shun; though never urged by me, he can achieve my desire!"[19] The will that was in *Rheingold* a quest for power is now destabilized by Alberich's opposing will. In supplement to his own will for power, Wotan now requires the will of another: "How can I create one, who, not through me, but on his own can achieve my will?"[20] The contest between patriarchs, between bourgeois and aristocrat, gives rise to the need for generativity. Siegfried and Hagen will continue to act on the wills of their fathers. But Wotan cannot create such a free man ("my hand can only make slaves!") and in despair his will changes its aim from power to self-destruction ("nur eines, will ich noch: das Ende, das Ende!"). Wotan is thereupon immediately confronted by the individual he wants to create but cannot. Yet he does not recognize the individual who fulfills his desire: his own daughter Brünnhilde, who defiantly chooses to do precisely what Wotan wills but cannot do.

In Act 3, Scenes 2 and 3, Wotan and Brünnhilde engage in an extraordinary exchange about Wotan's desire and her rebellious fulfillment of it. Wotan acknowledges Brünnhilde's special knowledge of his will: "Brünnhilde alone knew all my innermost secrets . . . saw to the depths of my spirit! Through her all my desires took shape in the world . . ."[21] Defying Wotan's explicit orders but acting on what she knew to be his deeper purpose, Brünnhilde is disinherited and condemned to the life of a housewife. But by disowning Brünnhilde he is creating the free person he thought he could not create, one who will destroy him and Valhalla. To disown Brünnhilde is also to disown that part of his will that she represents. In the interchange in Scene 3, Brünnhilde attempts to convince Wotan of this with only partial success. She was inspired to rebel against Wotan by the love she saw in Siegmund for Sieglinde, a love, she claims, that Wotan had implanted in Siegmund: "You, who this love in my heart inspired, when you inspired the Wälsung [Siegmund] with your will, you were not betrayed – though I broke your command."[22]

In the intensity of this father–daughter dialogue, the unconscious prevails. Each misrecognizes the other: Wotan does not see himself in Brünnhilde and she, thinking that she is following his true will, does not see that she in fact is its contradiction, even negation. Wotan, for his part, does acknowledge that he really wanted Brünnhilde to do what she did. Yet the rule breaking requires punishment, he insists. What he does not see is that the punishment will prove to be the condition for Brünnhilde's true independence, for her transformation from a god into a human, one who prefers finite love to the eternal glory of the gods. Asleep in a circle of flames, she will be awakened by Siegfried through whose love she will reconstitute her subjectivity from that of a goddess/aristocrat into a new species of humans who commit themselves to love and death. Brünnhilde, for her part, thinks she is carrying out Wotan's will for eternal power (his deepest will) when in fact she is setting into place the conditions for his demise (his unconscious will to self-destruction). What gives special pathos to this scene is Wagner's cunning understanding of the psycho-dynamics of father–daughter relations, of their unconscious incestuous desires, combined with the fateful world politics that hangs in the balance of the action.

For what emerges in *Siegfried*, during a quasi-therapeutic encounter between Erde and Wotan, is Wotan's will not to total power and not to self-destruction but to total power through self-destruction. His will is now to end the rule of the gods, along with the contest over patriarchy between himself (the aristocrat) and Alberich (the capitalist) in favor of world redemption and a free humanity that will be accomplished by Brünnhilde. "Know you what Wotan wills?" Wotan asks Erde. And answers himself, "That the gods may die soon gives me no anguish; I have willed that end! . . . today to the Wälsung [Siegfried and Brünnhilde] I have bequeathed my realm . . . Whatever may happen, the god will gladly yield his rule to the young!" [referring to Siegfried and Brünnhilde].[23] Wotan foresees that Brünnhilde "will achieve that deed that will free our world."[24] Immediately subsequent to this Wotan encounters Siegfried, who is on his way to Brünnhilde. Siegfried confronts Wotan and, in a scuffle, breaks his spear, indicating his independence from Wotan, his freedom, as well as Wotan's decline in power. This is the last time Wotan appears on stage in the *Ring*.

What, then, does Wotan want? Is his will (1) to live forever in Valhalla, ruling the world; or (2) merely to defend his rule against Alberich by maneuvering a hero (Siegfried) to accomplish what he cannot, i.e. return the Ring to the Rhinemaidens; or (3) to create a new humanity to redeem the world by a hero(ine)'s (Brünnhilde's) act of the destruction of the gods?

In the music dramas, the third choice appears to occur at least in part: Brünnhilde returns the Ring to the Rhine but, at the same time, this act destroys the gods. Since at this point Siegfried is dead, however, there is no chance that a new humanity, based on the free affirmation of finite love, will emerge. Wagner leaves us with an empty world, one without rulers and without any clear resolution. Boulez/Chereau substitute the audience for the absent new humanity. Before the curtain falls on *Götterdämmerung*, the camera draws back from the stage revealing an audience within the performance, one that has been deeply moved by the events before them. Amidst that audience a young blond girl turns from the stage to face the television audience, with those around her slowly joining her. A question is thus posed: will the audience now create the new humanity?

Boulez/Chereau adopt a revised Shavian interpretation of the *Ring* as a drama of social redemption: the class struggle between the nobles and bourgeoisie ends in the opportunity for a new free society. Shaw's interpretation[25] worked somewhat effectively up to the end of *Siegfried*: once Siegfried and Brünnhilde discover their love, the social drama is lost in favor of what Shaw calls "mere opera," which continues through *Götterdämmerung*. The Boulez/Chereau revision attempts to save the social interpretation by holding up the audience as the absent new humanity. The context of the composition of the *Ring* would favor this interpretation: a participant in the uprising of 1848 and a friend of Bakunin, Wagner wrote the work in a revolutionary mood. His intention concerning the first version of the work, *Siegfrieds Tod*, was to have a performance, tear down the hall and let the audience, now transformed, begin the process of social change.[26] Other interpreters judge Wagner's social views as too vague to serve as a program of reform, favoring a vague populism. In their view, Wagner was interested only in the German spirit as manifest in its folk tales, and that spirit was precisely characterized by its lack of social and political interest.[27]

The *Ring* and within it Wotan's will are often interpreted by reference to Wagner's changing allegiance to the philosophies of Feuerbach and Schopenhauer. Some critics argue that the work is basically a musical elaboration of Ludwig Feuerbach's social radicalism. If mankind were to reintegrate its alienated potentials, those which have been objectified into the God of Christianity, a revolution would take place in which the social bond and the human essence would be characterized by love.[28] Much can be made of the *Ring* when interpreted along these lines.[29] The love of Siegfried and

Brünnhilde, as well as the love of Siegmund and Sieglinde, which inspires Brünnhilde's rebellion against Wotan, may be said to instantiate a new humanity along Feuerbachian lines. In addition, the poem for the *Ring* was written in the early 1850s right after Wagner's participation in revolutionary politics.[30] From the Feuerbachian perspective, Wotan's will is the ineffectual will of the gods, a will open to revolutionary eclipse by human beings.[31] Those, like L. J. Rather, who see the *Ring* as an expression of Wagner's adherence to Arthur Schopenhauer's philosophy, point to Brünnhilde's self-immolation at the conclusion of the work, arguing that here is a representation not of Feuerbachian social revolution but of Schopenhauer's metaphysics of the will.[32] In this view, Wotan's will is a "dream of self-destruction," one that transcends the mere appearance of the world as representation toward a higher realization of the world as will. The actions of both Wotan and Brünnhilde, Rather maintains, are consistent with Wagner's turn to Schopenhauer, not as a change from revolutionary optimism to suicidal pessimism but as a change from the false egoism of emancipatory politics à la Feuerbach to a deeper integration of will and unconscious. The choice between Feuerbach and Schopenhauer is one between two blends of love and death. For Feuerbach death is an unfortunate limitation to the realization of love, whereas for Schopenhauer death is a condition for the fulfillment of love. Rather contends that the latter view most closely matches what occurs in the *Ring*.

There are serious problems with the Schopenhauerian interpretation of the *Ring*, some of which are "factual." The poem for the *Ring* was complete in printed form in early 1853, though the first performance was not given until 1876 and Wagner worked on the music almost until that date. Rather admits that Wagner did not study the writings of Schopenhauer until the mid-1850s, after the libretto of the *Ring* was finished.[33] He further admits that Wagner explicitly states that he did not read Schopenhauer's major work, *The World as Will and Representation*, until 1854. Then, in a crucial twist in his text, Rather vaguely alleges that Wagner was aware of Schopenhauer's philosophy as early as autumn 1852.[34] Rather could argue that even though Wagner had not studied Schopenhauer his work contains elements that conform to the philosopher's position. Yet he does not make this claim and instead attempts to force the "facts" to conform to his interpretation: he compulsively bends the temporal sequence of Wagner's reading in order to vindicate the intellectual historian's tenet that ideas must directly flow from one mind to another.

Rather even quotes a letter from Wagner to Röckel in which Wagner states that, at the time he wrote the *Ring*, he did not have the philosophical background (Schopenhauer's ideas) appropriate to it: "The most extraordinary thing in this connection I had to undergo at last with my Nibelung poem: I gave it shape at a time when I had, with my concepts alone, built up a Hellenistic-optimistic world the realization of which I held to be quite possible as soon as and if only human beings desired it. Doing so I rather ingeniously sought to help myself over the problem of why they did not in fact really want it."[35] Faced with this "contradiction" to his thesis of the linear influence of Schopenhauer's ideas on the *Ring*, Rather resorts to a most improbable solution: "Perhaps a buried remembrance of what Wagner had merely glanced at in passing [Schopenhauer's ideas on music] helped fertilize the soil in which the opening of *The Rhinegold* germinated and reached fruition."[36] Again the logocentric ideology of immediacy compels Rather to interpretative flights of fancy.

Rather's interpretation of the *Ring* through a supposed intellectual conversion of Wagner from Feuerbach to Schopenhauer is also betrayed by evidence of the continuing allegiance of Wagner up to the end of his life to anarchist attitudes against private property, evidence that Rather himself provides.[37] As in the case of Louis Althusser, who divided Marx's work into an early, bad Marx influenced by Hegel and a late, good Marx who resembled a scientific structuralist,[38] Rather is insistent on preserving patriarchal logocentrism by imposing a misleading intellectual break in Wagner's mind as the basis for interpreting the *Ring*.

These difficulties are characteristic of interpretations which derive from standard methods in intellectual history. Rather assumes that (1) Wagner's work is interpretable as a manifestation of his ideas and (2) that ideas may be analyzed as filiations from one thinker to another, as appropriations in which the appropriator takes an idea and perfectly assimilates it as his or her own. I want to argue that neither of these assumptions is adequate to the understanding of ideas or cultural works as discourses and as writing. These assumptions presume that ideas flow from the mind of one thinker to another in a form of identity. Instead I would argue that the mediations between the discourses and the form of writing itself inscribe disjunctions between the work of one author and another. Intellectual filiation, then, is much more like translation than repetition, in which the iteration incorporates material differences and is altered by them. Intellectual lineage is therefore not a smoothly functioning patriarchal process of insemination but a discursive dissemination, a complex blend of similarities and differences. Interpretive strategies that ignore this complexity reproduce an ideological reinforcement of patriarchal models of culture. Rather's "failure" to demonstrate the representation of Schopenhauer's philosophy in the *Ring* is thus not a simple falsehood but an affirmation of certain ideological inscriptions of culture.

Instead of interpreting Wotan's will by reference to the philosophical influences on Wagner, I believe a better reading emerges from a careful study of the text of the *Ring*. There are in the *Ring* three places where Wotan explicitly states his will. As I have shown above, these three enunciations are apparently contradictory: (1) an affirmation of eternal power and life in Valhalla; (2) a defensive, survivalist position against Alberich; and (3) a renunciation of power and acceptance of annihilation. There are two common characteristics of the three enunciations of will: they are all uttered to women and they are enunciated in or refer to unusual states of consciousness, like dreams. Will number 1 is spoken to Frika; Will number 2 is spoken to Brünnhilde; Will number 3 is spoken to Erda. These women are respectively Wotan's wife, daughter and lover. The question can be posed, why does Wotan reveal his will to women rather than to men, and why does he reveal his will to these women in particular?

As a beginning of an answer to this question, one can inquire as to the status of the masculine will in the *Ring*. It is fair to say that each instantiation of a masculine will in the work emerges as a failure, as a thwarted will. The male characters are, at one level, instances of the great masculine figures of Western culture: Alberich the entrepreneurial capitalist; Mime the artisan, scientist, engineer; Siegmund and Siegfried the warrior; Wotan the statesman; Fafner and Fasolt the peasant; the Nibelungs the workers; Loge the intellectual. Wagner's male characters explore the possibilities of masculinity and find themselves one and all in impasses. In the *Ring*, then, the male subject is at a point of confusion, a position from which no satisfactory direction may be discerned. Adorno, a critic not sympathetic to Wagner's music, praises him for his libretto on similar grounds:

> ... the libretto of the *Ring* ... treats the central underlying concerns of impending bourgeois decline, offering an example of the highly fertile relationship between musical form and the nature of the ideas which objectively determine this relationship.[39]

Adorno fails to note this decline in terms of gender.

But male figures are also in competition with one another. To the extent that each male character continues to have hope for the future, for the continuing viability of the figure of the subject they represent, each is in competition with the others. Men are locked in relations of force with one another. In this situation, one can only reveal one's true will to a woman, not to another man. And Wotan, the chief god, is no exception. When Nietzsche condemned Wagner's operas as little more than efforts to seduce women by flattering them, he failed to take account of Wagner's exploration of the dilemmas of modernity and the equivocal role of the male subject, in its various manifestations, within that context.[40]

From the standpoint of the male subject and its culture, women take the position of the other. When Wotan speaks to women he speaks not to competitors to his ego but to beings who are outside the context of male subject formations. He may address women not from the post-Oedipal position of the ego but from another place, a place that is more open to the heteronomies of desire and the unconscious. In the three statements of will, when Wotan speaks about his dreams, his female addressees are in positions of the Freudian analyst, as transferential figures who permit the unconscious to emerge, as others who authorize the appearance of desire and its progressive enunciation as self-consciousness. In these cases, Wotan's will is not an assertion of a post-Oedipal, masculine ego but an enunciation of a dream. Wotan moves in stages from dreaming of power, to dreaming of defending power, finally to dreaming that his power is powerless.

In Will number 1 Wotan tells Frika that he designed Valhalla "in dreams" which his "will brought to life."[41] At this point Wotan is confident that his masculine project of total control of the earth is still viable. Frika immediately brings Wotan back to reality: his project is bound up with competitive relations with other men so that its perfect realization is quixotic. The (Hegelian?) masculine model of the subject – idea followed by realization of idea – is arrogant folly.

In Will number 2 Wotan tells Brünnhilde that his will, now to protect the eternal glory of the gods from Alberich's designs for power, can be achieved only by a hero whom he creates but who is independent of him. He tells Brünnhilde that he has never revealed his will before, a statement which is false, and, far more interestingly, that his will can only take shape as he uses language to enunciate it. "These thoughts that I never have uttered, though I may think them, still they're unspoken. I think aloud, then, speaking to you."[42] After the delusory unity of Will number 1 has been revealed to Frika, Will number 2 only takes shape in its enunciation to the other, to a woman. The process of speech, in a performative mode, is now identical with the process of will formation. Wagner has moved from the confident (nineteenth-century) male subject to the hesitant, thera-peutic (twentieth-century) male subject. Wotan takes this step with trepidation: he fears loss of control. "If I should tell you, might I not lose the controlling power of my will?"[43] Yet he goes ahead and reveals/forms his will in his discourse to his daughter, the person, by the way, who will eventually destroy him, the person he regards as his alter ego and whom he disowns. Boulez/Chereau stress the psycho-analytic dimension of Wotan's speech by first suspending the circular movement of a pendulum that represents the ongoing course of events as controlled by Wotan, then by having Wotan remove an eye patch so that he appears without a mask, and finally having him look into a mirror so that he sees himself as he is.

For Wotan as for nineteenth-century men it is the paramour, not the analyst, to whom one speaks for true consolation and self-under-standing. And this mistress is Erda, the earth force and quintessential mother. Wotan goes to his lover/mother, approaching her for the final formulation of his will. This is a daring step on Wagner's part. The full male ego, the post-Oedipal subject, is in crisis and can resolve the crisis only by returning to the mother, regressing to the pre-Oedipal phase, a point before the ego took its mature shape, a point when the subject was unconscious and oneiric. Wotan takes this courageous step back toward the mother (he refers to Erda as "O mother") in quest of a connection with a bond that is irrevocably broken by the phallic phase when the father severs that earlier tie and the male child enters adulthood. To take this regressive/healing step, to make this move, is to destabilize the phallocentric form of the subject. And what Wotan discovers at the end of this process is that the modern patriar-chal male ego, the phallocentric subject, cannot be reconstituted but must be destroyed.

Wotan calls on Erda, awakening her from sleep and dreaming. He asks her advice ("say to me now: how a god can master his care?") and she responds, "You are not what you declare!"[44] Wotan is not the identical subject (god) he thinks he is. He restates and reinterprets what she said as, "You are not what you have dreamed," and goes on to ask, "Know you what Wotan wills?" But now this is a question that the other answers only when the ego places itself in her position. To paraphrase Lacan's revision of Freud: Where id (Wotan's) was, there shall ego (Erda's) be. By the process of transference with the lover/mother Wotan now understands *from her perspective* what he wills. "I have willed that end (of the gods and himself)!" he states. Erda's dream, as Wotan now sees ("dream of the gods' destruction"), is now his will ("Whatever may happen [he is no longer in control of the world's affairs], the god will gladly yield his rule to the young!"). Wotan now, in Will number 3, fully recognizes himself in the impasse of the male subject and can accept his fate only as one in which a new world, where there is no place for that subject, will overturn the old.

One may only speculate on the relation of Wotan to Wagner but certain lines of interpretation appear to be fruitful. Wagner dreamt of a total art work (*Gesamtkunstwerk*) in which he would realize the perfection of each of the arts, and, through the influence of the work on the audience, transform society. Like Wotan, then, Wagner dreams of total control, a male dream to be sure. But in the process of the inscription of that dream in the *Ring*, the unity of the male creative subject reveals its flaws and collapses.[45] Adorno contends that the total art work, along with other features of Wagner's work, are "emblems of Fascism." Adorno agrees that Wagner subverts the bourgeois ego but interprets this not as an indication of feminism but as an intimation of totalitarianism. Adorno writes, "Such defamations of the bourgeois [as Wotan's dismissing Hunding] . . . serve the same purpose as in the age of totalitarianism. . . . All that is intended is a dispensation from middle-class obligations. The insignificant are punished, while the prominent go scot-free. This is at any rate what happens in the *Ring*."[46]

Adorno's *In Search of Wagner*, a stunning polemic, sketches the portrait of an egomaniac. Wagner's personality and his music exude a lust for domination. The hyper-grandiose total art work is only the most obvious expression of a will to control and manipulate. The *Ring* of course is the most absurd extension of the total art work. "The *Ring* attempts," Adorno writes, "without much ado, nothing less than the encapsulation of the world process as a whole."[47] Wagner outdoes Hegel in self-inflation: he not only portrays the totality but does so in a totality. The political effect of Wagner's total art work, Adorno concludes, "is to warm up the alienated and reified relations of men [sic] and make them sound as if they were still human. . . . It combines the arts in order to produce an intoxicating brew."[48]

Surprisingly Adorno does not at all reject the motive of a total art work but claims that its fulfillment, its progressive realization as opposed to the "oceanic regression" of Wagner, can be attained only under socialism: "only in community, and in a mutual cooperation made possible thereby."[49] Just as Engels envisioned socialism as the fulfillment of bourgeois forms of romance and monogamy and the Frankfurt School in general see utopia as the completion of the autonomous bourgeois individual, so Adorno recuperates the total art work to his own politics. For me these are indicators that the critical theorist has not sufficiently differentiated himself from the object criticized. In particular it suggests that Adorno's disregard of the question of women in his evaluation of Wagner, however subtle and convincing his analysis of the musical elements of the *Ring*, is a step back behind Nietzsche, a regression in criticism. Without a feminist stance, the wrecks of the modern bourgeois ego as depicted in the *Ring* and perhaps as exemplified by Wagner himself appear only in the negative light of personal failure and fascist politics. The argument is then either ad hominum or anachronistic.

What, then, is the relation between Wagner, who would control the world through his art, and Wotan, who recognizes that such control is impossible? There can be no final answer to this question, except to the extent that it is instantiated in productions of the *Ring*. Boulez/Chereau perhaps face the issue at the end of *Götterdämmerung* by having a young girl in the audience within the play, as we have seen, rise first and turn to the viewing audience, a gesture which risks sentimentality but which also suggests that the binary contradiction of Wotan/Wagner can be carried further only by the audience. Wagner's will for the total art work is thus incomplete, open in its determination like all works of art, until it is taken over (internalized/transformed) by an audience, an audience whose characteristics and responses no artist can anticipate and control. Like Nietzsche's dancing star, the new values are inscribed in history by working through the old values, the will of Wotan. Like all artists, Wagner, in the *Ring*, inscribes his own will so that it may be acted upon and overcome by its audience.

In this sense, despite all of Wagner's efforts to control and manipulate the audience, his work places him in the same position that Wotan takes in speaking to Frika/Brünnhilde/Erda, in a psychoanalytic, feminist position of accepting alterity, the non-identity of the subject. This acceptance was certainly ambivalent, as Wagner and Wotan betray the male project of autonomy and control while at the same time placing destiny in the hands of the audience for the former and women for the latter.

10

War in the Mode of
Information

Several aspects of the representation of the US–Iraq War arrested my attention. These were (1) the role of environmental issues, (2) the concern for historic and cultural monuments, (3) the presence of coalition media personnel in Iraq subsequent to the outbreak of hostilities, and (4) the "real time" transmission of images and sound from the theater of operations, transforming the battlefield into a theater. I believe these phenomena were without precedent in war and therefore deserve special consideration.

The oil spill in the Persian Gulf was presented by the Bush administration as a deliberate sabotage of nature by Saddam Hussein. Rather than an accident of the shipping industry or a hazard of petroleum technology, this spill was attributed to the maniacal intentions of a despot. Suddenly a new criterion was imposed on the conduct of war: the preservation of the environment. War, considered the ultimate state of the polis at least since Plato, the true test of the moral fiber of the community, was now, by dint of US administration spokesmen, a limited action, one carried out with constraints imposed by "higher" considerations, such as the environment. When the US air force destroyed one-third of the forests of Vietnam by defoliants, napalm and assorted chemicals invented by distinguished American scientists and produced by some of its leading corporations, the Johnson and Nixon administrations deemed the environment a secondary concern in comparison with the pursuit of military goals. Now such a hierarchy of values is conveniently reversed: nature stands above American war aims and strategy, an inviolable temple befouled only by Hitlerian regimes, not civilized nations. I wonder if the administration would maintain this order of values if New York and Washington, DC, were subject to the plight then endured by Baghdad and Basra. Or, has mankind, as represented by the Bush administration, come truly to realize that the preservation of the Earth is more important than the transitory ambitions of nation-states.

In the same spirit the Bush administration consistently upheld a touching regard for Islamic religious sites and cultural treasures, and, just as surprisingly, for what it deemed irreplaceable archaeological monuments. These fortunate islands of human expression were exempt from aerial bombardment. They were so high in the scheme of Bush's values that even when they housed Iraqi military materials they remained unscathed. One might cynically conjecture that Bush was motivated not by esteem for Arab culture but by fear of Arab popular sentiment. To violate the shrines of Islam was to risk Arab defection from the United Nations coalition. Or, even worse, to violate the remains of the "cradle of civilization" in the Tigris and Euphrates would have incited the opposition of all mankind. The historic treasures that happened to be located in modern-day Iraq had to be kept safe from the happenstance of war. Here again one might ask about the monuments of Dresden or Hiroshima or Nagasaki. In the long list of the crimes of Hitler one rarely finds a complaint that the V-2 bombs might have pulverized British monuments or treasures, many of which, to be sure, were the booty of its imperialism of an earlier epoch. Yet in 1991, beautiful objects and edifices were immune from destruction by warring nations. Again is there just a scintilla, amidst the barrage of rhetoric and tactics, of a relativization of war with respect to the awesome beauty of historic cultures?

In early August 1990 a small army of news correspondents plied their trade in Iraq. When the war began, they were not immediately forced to leave the country even though they mostly represented coalition nations in armed combat against Iraq. Certain of them remained after two months of brutal aerial assault. I am not aware that either of these circumstances existed in previous states of war. The continuation of CNN's presence may be attributed to Hussein's propaganda methods and the dilatory eviction of other journalists may be accounted for by his lack of efficiency. Even taking these arguments into account the exceptional nature of the situation should not be overlooked. Enemy journalists, even if heavily censored by the regime, are not usually permitted to continue their broadcasts in a hostile nation. This anomaly suggests to me that worldwide opinion has become a significant factor in warfare, and it has become so due to the ascendant role of the media in politics more generally. There now is set in place a network of information flows that instantaneously transmits on a global basis. Such a communications system may no longer be interrupted even in a state of war. American communications satellites read license plates of vehicles in Baghdad. Under these conditions, lesser nations have no choice but to hook into the circuits as best they can, regardless of which nation owns or controls those technologies. In yet a third way, warfare has changed perhaps forever.

Of all the novelties of the US–Iraq conflict the most interesting to me was the instantaneous transmission from the site of conflict to the living rooms in America and the world. In the first few days of the war, before the American military attained control over the journalists, Americans were treated to an unprecedented transmission of sights and sounds from the war front as they occurred. Of course, news people were restricted in their movement in Israel, Saudi Arabia and Iraq. There is no question of a panoptic transmission of all important information. Yet enough was captured by audio and video technology to provide viewers with a "you are there" experience. And America was glued to the tube, no doubt about that. The weird, bizarre phenomenon of a nation of hundreds of millions, a superbowl audience, watching a war on television and listening on radio during rush hours as it actually unfolded gives one pause.

And yet the media that transformed the war theater into a theater of war did not provide a transparent representation of reality. In the mode of information electronically mediated communication transfigures language and images in startlingly new ways. No rhetoric of realism captures the new communication situation. The sense of being there was figured through powerful framing devices that subverted realism as it enacted it, a doubling message system if ever there was one. First, television coverage of the war gave the impression of news people as participants, hurriedly donning their gas masks to the effect that the illusion of realism was forced into suspension. In previous wars, World War II, Korea and Vietnam, news people strove for the voice of the omniscient narrator or Olympian observer, removing themselves as much as possible from presenting to the audience their plight as that of vulnerable targets of enemy bullets, grenades and artillery fire, from presenting news gathering as news itself. Not in

Iraq: here the messengers were the messages. The fate of journalists was every bit as much part of the news as the fate of soldiers and civilians. The news became systematically self-reflexive. As the audience was transported to the scene of operations, the vehicle of transmission itself became part of the operation and the story.

Second, the television image combines simulation with verisimilitude, irreality with intimacy. Comfortably ensconced in one's home, the viewer listens on a small pretty colored screen to familiar figures who speak in reassuring tones. The TV, with its image, becomes a piece of furniture, friendly and familiar, if not part of the family itself, then a friend who visits frequently. The activity of watching television, repeated so often for so many years, is a habit that contributes to its reality effect. And the images themselves, so lifelike and convincing, so much like what the eye perceives, and therefore so authoritative, are so easy to believe. Faces of Israelis and Saudis and Iraqis, detailed charts of military hardware, reports from over-decorated generals, from people with strange accents and from points all over the world, a barrage of images and information, packaged in easy-to-take portions, punctuated by commercial breaks where powerful fantasies flow by too quickly – the world has truly been faxed, cabled, express delivered.

But then the screen flashes with scud rockets exploding over Tel Aviv and one has a sense of *déjà vu*: this is just like some Nintendo game one has seen one's nephew play. And then a week or two later, a deep voice intones something about an actual destruction of a military installation while the screen becomes a bomber's view of its target, with the hair lines homing in on some building, concluding with a flash on the screen. Another *déjà vu*: the computer game of flight simulator and the air war in Iraq are much the same. The heightened realism of seeing the war from the bomb's point of view and the idle fantasy of a computer game merge into the same image. Or better, as television attempts to convince the viewer with absolute certainty of the efficacy of the air war, as it places him/her on the nose of the bomb and takes him/her on its flight to its target as if you the viewer, with Superman's fists, were smashing the enemy to bits, as, in other words, the information you are given is overwhelmingly convincing down to the least detail so that belief in the government's policy and the military's effectiveness are totally beyond doubt, just when you are taken to the place of impact, the intensifying rhetoric of realism implodes into the hyper-realism of computer games. After all, you really were not at the point of impact; the target on the screen did look like a building, but what sort of building? The voice over called it a military target but it could have been a school, or a warehouse full of computer games. And of course there is no way to know when the footage on the screen was taped or filmed. It could have been made in a military training camp in North Carolina or in a Hollywood studio. The more television images attempt to convince the viewer of the reference to reality the more the image itself becomes the reality. This is the simulation effect of television, its iron law that no general can dislodge from its rhetorical position.

And yet the nation, if the polls are to be believed, was overwhelmingly convinced. Why is this? The generals must have felt satisfied with their television strategy, if not with their military campaign. From the outset of the military's censorship of the images televised back home, Americans were assured that the experience of the Vietnam War would not be repeated. The generals were speaking here not so much of the military defeat in Vietnam, not so much of the alleged constraint imposed by the politicians on the conduct of that war, but of its television strategy. No more body counts, that was a mistake, we were told. And no more images of dying American soldiers, no more front-line scenes of skirmishes with bullets flying and men screaming in their death throes. Iraq would be a sanitized war. Perhaps. I would say that Iraq was a high tech, high "information" war, just as we saw with the image from the bomb's point of view. The army's television show, with its daily segments of sorties and patriot anti-missile successes, with its sortie counts instead of body counts, was a soap opera war where "information" was the leading character and support for the war the discursive effect.

Notes

Notes to Chapter 1: Social Theory and the New Media

1 See also, for a discussion of theories of the media, Armand Mattelart and Michèle Mattelart, *Rethinking Media Theory*, trans. James Cohen and Marina Urquidi (Minneapolis: University of Minnesota Press, 1992).

2 For the best statement of this position, see Ernesto Laclau and Chantal Mouffe, *Hegemony and Socialist Strategy: Towards a Radical Democratic Politics*, trans. Winston Moore and Paul Cammack (London: Verso, 1985), especially chapter 3.

3 From *Scènes de la vie future* (1930), as quoted by Walter Benjamin in "The Work of Art in the Age of Mechanical Reproduction," *Illuminations*, trans. Harry Zohn (New York: Schocken, 1969), p. 239.

4 Pierre Bourdieu, *Distinction: A Social Critique of the Judgment of Taste*, trans. Richard Nice (Cambridge, MA: Harvard University Press, 1984).

5 Theodor Adorno and Max Horkheimer, *Dialectic of Enlightenment*, trans. John Cumming (New York: Continuum, 1972).

6 For another understanding of Adorno's relation to technology and mass culture, see Fredric Jameson, *Late Marxism, or, the Persistence of the Dialectic* (New York: Verso, 1990), and Martin Jay, *Adorno* (London: Fontana, 1984).

7 Theodor Adorno, "Television and the Patterns of Mass Culture," *Quarterly of Film, Radio and Television*, vol. 8 (1954),

p. 216.

8 Theodor Adorno, "On the Fetish-Character in Music and the Regression of Listening," in Andrew Arato and Paul Breines, eds, *The Essential Frankfurt School Reader* (New York: Urizen, 1978), pp. 270–99. For a more appreciative reading of Adorno's work on music, see Edward Said, *Musical Elaborations* (New York: Columbia University Press, 1991).

9 John Mowitt, "The Sound of Music in the Era of its Electronic Reproducibility," in Richard Leppert and Susan McClary, eds, *Music and Society* (New York: Cambridge University Press, 1987), pp. 173–97.

10 This theme is explored by Andreas Huyssen in "Mass Culture as Woman: Modernisms's Other," in Tania Modleski, ed., *Studies in Entertainment: Critical Approaches to Mass Culture* (Bloomington: Indiana University Press, 1986), pp. 188–208.

11 Theodor Adorno, "The Curves of the Needle," trans. Thomas Levin, *October*, 55 (Winter 1990), p. 50.

12 Theodor Adorno, "The Form of the Phonograph Record," trans. Thomas Levin, *October*, 55 (Winter 1990), pp. 58–9.

13 Theodor Adorno, "Opera and the Long-Playing Record," *October*, 55 (Winter 1990), pp. 62–6.

14 Thomas Levin, "Music in the Age of its Technological Reproducibility," *October*, 55 (Winter 1990), p. 47.

15 *Minima Moralia: Reflections from a Damaged Life*, trans. E. Jephcott (London: New Left Books, 1974), pp. 15–16.

16 Ibid., p. 18.

17 Ibid., p. 55.

18 Paul Virilio, *War and Cinema: The Logistics of Perception*, trans. Patrick Camiller (New York: Verso, 1989), p. 20.

19 Mark Poster, *The Mode of Information* (Cambridge: Polity Press; Chicago: University of Chicago Press, 1990).

20 Louis Althusser, "Ideology and Ideological State Apparatuses" (1970), trans. Ben Brewster in *Lenin and Philosophy and Other Essays* (London: New Left Books, 1971), p. 146.

21 Jürgen Habermas, *The Structural Transformation of the Public Sphere*, trans. Thomas Burger (Cambridge: Polity Press; Cambridge, MA: MIT Press, 1989), p. 245.

22 Jürgen Habermas, *The Theory of Communicative Action*, vol. 2: *Lifeworld and System: A Critique of Functionalist Reason*, trans. Thomas McCarthy (Cambridge: Polity Press; Boston: Beacon Press, 1987), p. 184.

23 Jürgen Habermas, *The Theory of Communicative Action*, p. 390.
24 Walter Benjamin, "The Work of Art in the Age of Mechanical Reproduction," trans. Harry Zohn in *Illuminations*, ed. Hannah Arendt (New York: Schocken, 1969), pp. 217–51.
25 For Adorno's critique of "The Work of Art," see his letter to Benjamin in Rodney Livingstone et al., eds, *Aesthetics and Politics*, trans. Ronald Taylor et al. (London: New Left Books, 1977), pp. 120–6.
26 For an excellent treatment of Benjamin, see Susan Buck-Morss, *The Dialectics of Seeing: Walter Benjamin and the Arcades Project* (Cambridge, MA: MIT Press, 1991), especially pp. 124–5ff on the relation of art and technology in Benjamin. Buck-Morss also shows how the Arcades project repeats Benjamin's thesis in the "Work of Art" essay concerning the relation of art and technology in film (p. 268).
27 On this theoretical problem, see Constance Penley and Andrew Ross, eds, *Technoculture* (Minneapolis: University of Minnesota Press, 1991).
28 Hans Magnus Enzensberger, "Constituents of a Theory of Media," in Critical Essays (New York: Continuum, 1982), pp. 47–8, 52. First published in *New Left Review* in 1970.
29 Jean Baudrillard, "The Ecstasy of Communication," in Hal Foster, ed., *The Anti-Esthetic* (Port Townsend, WA: Bay Press, 1983), p. 130.
30 Jean Baudrillard, *Amérique* (Paris: Grasset, 1986). Here Baudrillard too often descends into the stance of the defensive European visitor.
31 *Jean Baudrillard: Selected Writings*, ed. Mark Poster (Cambridge: Polity Press; Stanford: Stanford University Press, 1988), p. 217.
32 Jean Baudrillard, "Requiem for the Media," in *For a Critique of the Political Economy of the Sign*, trans. Charles Levin (St Louis: Telos Press, 1981), pp. 169ff.
33 See, for example, Andreas Huyssen, "Mass Culture as Woman: Modernism's Other," in Tania Modleski, ed., *Studies in Entertainment: Critical Approaches to Mass Culture* (Bloomington: Indiana University Press, 1986), pp. 188–208, and Douglas Kellner, *Jean Baudrillard: From Marxism to Postmodernism and Beyond* (Cambridge: Polity Press; Stanford: Stanford University Press, 1989), pp. 214ff.

34   *Dialectic of Enlightenment*, p. 157.
35   Félix Guattari, "Regimes, Pathways, Subjects," trans. Brian Massumi in Jonathan Crary and Sanford Kwinter, eds, *Zone 6: Incorporations* (Cambridge, MA: MIT Press, 1992), p. 18. See also Donna Haraway, "The Promises of Monsters: A Regenerative Politics for Inappropriate/d Others," in Lawrence Grossberg et al., eds, *Cultural Studies* (New York: Routledge, 1992), pp. 295–337.
36   Georges Canguilhem, "Machine and Organism," trans. Mark Cohen and Randall Cherry in *Incorporations*, p. 45.
37   Hillel Schwartz, "Torque: The New Kinaesthetic," in *Incorporations*, p. 104.
38   Manuel DeLanda, "Nonorganic Life," in *Incorporations*, pp. 129–67.
39   Félix Guattari, "Machinic Heterogenesis," trans. James Creech in Verena Conley, ed., *Rethinking Technologies* (Minneapolis: University of Minnesota Press, 1993), p. 16.
40   See a fascinating essay on the theme of the interface by Brenda Laurel, *Computers as Theatre* (New York: Addison-Wesley, 1991).
41   Teresa de Lauretis, *Technologies of Gender* (Bloomington: Indiana University Press, 1987).
42   See, for example, John Hartley, *Tele-ology: Studies in Television* (London: Routledge, 1992).

Notes to Chapter 2:   Postmodern Virtualities

1   See Jean-Christophe Agnew, *Worlds Apart: The Market and the Theater in Anglo-American Thought, 1550–1750* (New York: Cambridge University Press, 1986), for an analysis of the formation of this subject position and its particular relation to the theater. Jürgen Habermas, in *The Structural Transformation of the Public Sphere*, trans. Thomas Burger (Cambridge: Polity Press; Cambridge, MA: MIT Press, 1989), offers a "public sphere" of coffee houses, salons and other agora-like locations as the arena of the modern subject, while Max Weber, in *The Protestant Ethic and the Spirit of Capitalism*, trans. Talcott Parsons (New York: Macmillan, 1958), looks to Calvinist religion for the roots of the same phenomenon.
2   See, for example, the discussion of new "interactive" technologies in the *New York Times* on December 19, 1993. In "The

Uncertain Promises of Interactivity," Calvin Sims restricts future innovations to movies on demand, on-line information services, interactive shopping, "participatory programming," video games and conferencing systems for business (p. 6F). He omits electronic mail and its possible expansion to sound and image in networked virtual reality systems.

3 I have not discussed the work of Marshall McLuhan simply for lack of space and also because it is not as directly related to traditions of critical social theory as is Benjamin's, Enzensberger's and Baudrillard's. Also of interest is Friedrich Kittler's "Gramophone, Film, Typewriter," *October*, 41 (1987–8), pp. 101–18, and *Discourse Networks: 1800/1900*, trans. Michael Metteer (Stanford: Stanford University Press, 1990).

4 For an excellent essay on the economics of the Internet and its basic structural features, see Hal Varian, "Economic FAQs About the Internet," which is available on the Internet at listserver@essential.org (send message: subscribe tap-info [your name]) and in the Fall 1994 issue of *Journal of Economic Perspectives*.

5 Kevin Cooke and Dan Lehrer, "The Whole World is Talking," *The Nation* (July 12, 1993), p. 61.

6 Philip Elmer-Dewitt, "Take a Trip into the Future on the Electronic Superhighway," *Time* (April 12, 1993), p. 52.

7 George Gilder, "Telecosm: the New Rule of Wireless," *Forbes ASAP* (March 29, 1993), p. 107.

8 David Bollier, "The Information Superhighway: Roadmap for Renewed Public Purpose," *Tikkun* 8: 4 (1993), p. 22. See also the cautionary tone of Herbert Schiller in "The 'Information Highway': Public Way or Private Road?," *The Nation* (July 12, 1993), pp. 64–6.

9 Mitchell Kapor, "Where Is the Digital Highway Really Heading?: The Case for a Jeffersonian Information Policy," *Wired* 1: 3 (1993), p. 55.

10 For the implications of the Internet on world affairs, see Majid Tehranian, "World With/Out Wars: Moral Spaces and the Ethics of Transnational Communication," *The Public* (Ljubljana) forthcoming.

11 For one report, see Craig Turner, "Courts Gag Media at Sensational Canada Trial," *Los Angeles Times* (May 15, 1994), p. A4.

12 Robert Lee Hotz, "Computer Code's Security Worries Privacy Watchdogs," *Los Angeles Times* (October 4, 1993), pp. A3, 22.

13 Many writers prefer the term "artificial reality" precisely be-

cause they want to underscore the privilege of real reality. Needless to say this substitution will not cure the problem.

14 Julian Dibbell, "A Rape in Cyberspace," *The Village Voice* (December 21, 1993), pp. 36–42. I am indebted to Rob Kling for making me aware of this piece.

15 Carolyn Marvin, *When Old Technologies Were New: Thinking About Electric Communication in the Late Nineteenth Century* (New York: Oxford University Press, 1988), especially pp. 222ff.

16 For interesting examinations of this practice, see Mark Dery, ed., "Flame Wars: The Discourse of Cyberculture," *South Atlantic Quarterly* 92: 4 (1993).

17 Howard Rheingold, "A Slice of Life in my Virtual Community," in Linda Harasim, ed., *Global Networks: Computers and International Communication* (Cambridge, MA: MIT Press, 1993), p. 61.

18 See Rheingold's comments, for example: ". . . I believe [virtual communities] are in part a response to the hunger for community that has followed the disintegration of traditional communities around the world" ("Virtual Community," p. 62).

19 See Benedict Anderson, *Imagined Community: Reflections on the Origin and Spread of Nationalism* (New York: Verso, 1983).

20 Jean-Luc Nancy, *The Inoperative Community*, trans. Peter Conner et al. (Minneapolis: University of Minnesota Press, 1991), p. xxxviii. See also the response by Maurice Blanchot in *The Unavowable Community*, trans. Pierre Joris (Barrytown, NY: Station Hill Press, 1988).

21 Allucquère Roseanne Stone, "Virtual Systems," in *Incorporations*, ed. Jonathan Crary and Stanford Kwinter (Cambridge, MA: MIT Press, 1992), p. 618.

22 Jon Katz, "The Tales They Tell in Cyber-Space are a Whole Other Story," *Los Angeles Times* (January 23, 1994), p. 2: 1.

23 See *Mondo 2,000*, 11 (1993), pp. 34 and 106.

24 Jean-François Lyotard, *The Postmodern Condition: A Report on Knowledge*, trans. Geoff Bennington and Brian Massumi (Minneapolis: University of Minnesota Press, 1984), p. xxiv.

25 N. Katherine Hayles, "The Seductions of Cyberspace," in Varena Conley, ed., *Rethinking Technologies* (Minneapolis: University of Minnesota Press, 1993), p. 175.

26 Claudia Springer in "The Pleasure of the Interface," *Screen* 32: 3 (1991), pp. 303–23, is especially insightful on this question.

27 Katherine Hayles, "Virtual Bodies and Flickering Signifiers," *October* 66 (Fall 1993), pp. 69–91, interprets these "different configurations of embodiment, technology and culture" through the binary pattern/randomness rather than presence/absence.

28 For an excellent statement of this problem, see Rey Chow, *Writing Diaspora* (Bloomington: Indiana University Press, 1993), especially chapters 1 and 2. See also an important alternative view in David Lloyd, "Ethnic Cultures, Minority Discourse and the State," in Peter Hulme, ed., *Colonial Discourse/ Postcolonial Theory* (Manchester: Manchester University Press, 1994), pp. 221–38.

29 Karl Marx, "On the Jewish Question," in Robert Tucker, ed., *The Marx–Engels Reader* (New York: Norton, 1978), pp. 26–52.

Notes to Chapter 3: Postmodernity and the Politics of Multiculturalism

1 Jean-François Lyotard, *The Postmodern Condition: A Report on Knowledge*, trans. Geoff Bennington and Brian Massumi (Minneapolis: University of Minnesota Press, 1984), p. 15.

2 Jürgen Habermas, *The Philosophical Discourse of Modernity: Twelve Lectures*, trans. Frederick Lawrence (Cambridge: Polity Press; Cambridge, MA: MIT Press, 1987).

3 Ibid., p. 296.

4 Seminar at University of California, Irvine, 1988.

5 *The Postmodern Condition*, p. 82. Philippe Lacoue-Labarthe in "Talks," *Diacritics* 14: 3 (1984) refers to Habermas as a "dinosaur from the *Aufklärung*" (p. 25).

6 Seyla Benhabib, "Epistemologies of Postmodernism: A Rejoinder to Jean-François Lyotard," in Linda Nicholson, ed., *Feminism/Postmodernism* (New York: Routledge, 1990), pp. 107–30.

7 Jürgen Habermas, "Taking Aim at the Heart of the Present," in *The New Conservatism: Cultural Criticism and the Historians' Debate*, trans. Shierry Weber Nicholsen (Cambridge: Polity Press; Cambridge, MA: MIT Press, 1989), pp. 173–9.

8 Jürgen Habermas, "Modernity, an Incomplete Project," *The Anti-Aesthetic: Essays in Postmodern Culture*, ed. Hal Foster (Port Townsend, WA: Bay Press, 1983), p. 8.

9   This position is fully developed in Habermas's magnum opus *The Theory of Communicative Action*, vol. 1: *Reason and the Rationalization of Society*, trans. Thomas McCarthy (Cambridge: Polity Press; Boston: Beacon, 1984), and vol. 2: *Lifeworld and System: A Critique of Functionalist Reason*, trans. Thomas McCarthy (Cambridge: Polity Press; Boston: Beacon, 1987).

10 Jürgen Habermas, *The Structural Transformation of the Public Sphere: An Inquiry into a Category of Bourgeois Society*, trans. Thomas Burger (Cambridge: Polity Press; Cambridge, MA: MIT Press, 1989), p. 163.

11 Arjun Appadurai, "Disjuncture and Difference in the Global Cultural Economy," in *Public Culture* 2: 2 (1990), p. 10.

12 *The Structural Transformation of the Public Sphere*, pp. 170–1, 175, 179, 164.

13 On this question, see Peter Miller, *Domination and Power* (London: Routledge & Kegan Paul, 1987).

14 Seyla Benhabib, "Epistemologies of Postmodernism: A Rejoinder to Jean-François Lyotard," in Linda Nicholson, ed., *Feminism/Postmodernism* (New York: Routledge, 1990), pp. 107–30.

15 See Linda Nicholson, ed., *Feminism/Postmodernism* (New York: Routledge, 1990).

16 For example, see Meaghan Morris, "Postmodernity and Lyotard's Sublime," *The Pirate's Fiancée: Feminism, Reading Postmodernism* (New York: Verso, 1988), pp. 223–40. For a positive view of the same position, see John Hinkson, "Postmodernism and Structural Change," *Public Culture* 2: 2 (1990), p. 84.

17 Dick Hebdige characterizes these standard themes as totalization, telos and utopia in *Hiding in the Light: On Images and Things* (New York: Routledge, 1988), pp. 186–98.

18 Ernesto Laclau and Chantal Mouffe, *Hegemony and Socialist Strategy: Towards a Radical Democratic Politics*, trans. Winston Moore and Paul Cammack (London: Verso, 1985), chapter 3.

19 In this connection, see Jean-François Lyotard, "The Sublime and the Avant-Garde," trans. Lisa Liebman, *Paragraph* 6: 2 (1985), pp. 1–18, and "Sensus Communis," trans. Marian Hobson and Geoff Bennington, *Paragraph* 11: 1 (1988), pp. 1–23.

20 Jean-François Lyotard, in *The Differend: Phrases in Dispute*, trans. Georges van den Abbeele (Minneapolis: University of

Minnesota Press, 1988), presents a minimalist argument for critique.

21   Jean-François Lyotard, *The Inhuman: Reflections on Time*, trans. Geoff Bennington and Rachel Bowlby (Cambridge: Polity, 1992), especially chapters 5, 7, 8. See also his "The Wall, the Gulf and the Sun: A Fable," in Mark Poster, ed., *Politics, Theory and Contemporary Culture* (New York: Columbia University Press, 1993), pp. 261–76.

22   Donna Haraway, *Simians, Cyborgs and Women: The Re-Invention of Nature* (New York: Routledge, 1991).

23   Tom Bridges, "Multiculturalism as a Postmodernist Project," *Postmodern Culture*. This journal is distributed electronically and may be received by electronic mail by sending a message to pmc-talk@ncsuvm. The filename is bridges essay 1.

24   Michel Foucault, "Two Lectures," in Colin Gordon, ed., *Power/ Knowledge*, trans. Colin Gordon et al. (New York: Pantheon, 1980), p. 83.

25   I am referring to the important collection edited by Lawrence Grossberg, Cary Nelson and Paula Treicher, entitled simply *Cultural Studies* (New York: Routledge, 1992). Most of the essays confront the issue of essentialist agency in the context of multiculturalism, though that term is not often used. See, for example, Tony Bennet, "Putting Policy into Cultural Studies," p. 31; Homi Bhabha, "Postcolonial Authority and Postmodern Guilt," p. 57; Angie Chabram-Dernersesian, "I Throw Punches for My Race . . . ," p. 85.

26   Homi Bhabha has articulated most fully the dilemma of minority subject positions. He writes, for example, that "The marginal or 'minority' is not the space of a celebratory, or utopian, self-marginalization" ("Introduction," in Homi Bhabha, ed., *Nation and Narration* [New York: Routledge, 1990], p. 4). His concept of hybridity is an effort to expose the complexity of non-Western (and Western) subject positions.

Notes to Chapter 4:   The Mode of Information and Postmodernity

1   Mark Poster, *The Mode of Information* (Cambridge: Polity Press; Chicago: University of Chicago Press, 1990).

2   Elizabeth Eisenstein, *The Printing Press as an Agent of Change*

(New York: Cambridge University Press, 1980).

3 Jean-François Lyotard, *Inhuman*, trans. Geoff Bennington and Rachel Bowlby (Cambridge: Polity Press, 1992).

4 J. Hillis Miller, "The Work of Cultural Criticism in the Age of Digital Reproduction," in *Illustration* (Cambridge, MA: Harvard University Press, 1992).

5 Jean Baudrillard, *Selected Writings*, ed. Mark Poster, trans. Jacques Mourrain (Stanford: Stanford University Press, 1988).

6 Joshua Meyrowitz, *No Sense of Place: The Impact of Electronic Media on Social Behavior* (New York: Oxford University Press, 1985).

7 Michel Foucault, *Discipline and Punish: The Birth of the Prison*, trans. Alan Sheridan (New York: Pantheon, 1977).

8 Michael Heim, *Electric Language: A Philosophical Study of Word Processing* (New Haven: Yale University Press, 1987).

9 George Landow, *Hypertext: The Convergence of Contemporary Critical Theory and Technology* (Baltimore: Johns Hopkins University Press, 1992).

10 Jay Bolter, *Writing Space: The Computer, Hypertext, and the History of Writing* (Hillsdale, NJ: Lawrence Erlbaum Associates, 1991).

11 Richard Lanham, "The Electronic Word: Literary Study and the Digital Revolution," *New Literary History* 20: 2 (1989), pp. 265–90.

12 Marie Marchand, *La Grande aventure du Minitel* (Paris: Larousse, 1987).

13 Andrew Feenberg, "Computer Conferencing and the Humanities," *Instructional Science* 16 (1987), pp. 169–86.

14 Roxanne Starr Hiltz and Murray Turoff, *The Network Nation: Human Communication via Computer* (London: Addison-Wesley, 1978).

15 Jacques Derrida, *Of Grammatology*, trans. Gayatri Spivak (Baltimore: Johns Hopkins University Press, 1976).

16 Jacques Derrida, *Postcard: From Socrates to Freud and Beyond*, trans. Alan Bass (Chicago: University of Chicago Press, 1987).

17 Norbert Wiener, *The Human Use of Human Beings* (New York: Anchor, 1954).

18 Louis Althusser, "Ideology and Ideological State Apparatuses," in *Lenin and Philosophy and Other Essays*, trans. Ben Brewster (London: New Left Books, 1971).

19 John Hinkson, "Marxism, Postmodernism and Politics Today," *Arena* 94 (1991), pp. 138–66.

Notes to Chapter 5: Databases as Discourse, or Electronic Interpellations

1 I shall be concerned not with all databases but only with those that have fields for individuals. Thus inventory databases, for example, are excluded from my discussion.

2 Herbert Schiller, *Who Knows: Information in the Age of the Fortune 500* (New York: Ablex, 1981); and Timothy Luke and Stephen White, "Critical Theory, the Informational Revolution, and an Ecological Path to Modernity," in John Forester, ed., *Critical Theory and Public Life* (Cambridge, MA: MIT Press, 1985), pp. 22–53.

3 David Burnham, *The Rise of the Computer State* (New York: Random House, 1983); James B. Rule, *Private Lives and Public Surveillance: Social Control in the Computer Age* (New York: Schocken, 1974); and Gary Marx, *Undercover: Police Surveillance in America* (Berkeley: University of California Press, 1988).

4 The concept of "interpellation" entered the arena of critical theory with Althusser's essay "Ideology and Ideological State Apparatuses" (1970), trans. Ben Brewster in *Lenin and Philosophy and Other Essays* (London: New Left Books, 1971), pp. 160ff, where the Marxist concept of ideology was presented as the interpellating agent. See also Kaja Silverman, *The Subject of Semiotics* (New York: Oxford, 1983) for an excellent discussion of the concept of interpellation.

5 Michel Foucault, *The Archaeology of Knowledge*, trans. A. M. Sheridan Smith (New York: Pantheon, 1966), pp. 54–5.

6 Manfred Frank, "On Foucault's Concept of Discourse," in François Ewald, ed., *Michel Foucault, Philosopher*, trans. Timothy Armstrong (New York: Routledge, 1992), p. 110.

7 Michel Foucault, "The Question of Method," in Graham Burchell et al., eds, *The Foucault Effect: Studies in Governmentality*, various translators (Chicago: University of Chicago Press, 1991), p. 79.

8 Michel Foucault, "An Aesthetics of Existence," in Lawrence

Kritzman, ed., *Foucault: Politics, Philosophy, Culture*, trans. Alan Sheridan et al. (New York: Routledge, 1988), pp. 50–1.

9 Michel Foucault, *The History of Sexuality*, vol. I: *An Introduction*, trans. Robert Hurley (New York: Pantheon, 1978), pp. 129–31.

10 *Discipline and Punish: The Birth of the Prison*, trans. Alan Sheridan (New York: Pantheon, 1977), p. 139.

11 Ibid., p. 177.

12 Along similar lines, Gilles Deleuze suggests that we have changed from a disciplinary society to a society of control. See his "Postscript on the Societies of Control," *October* 59 (Winter 1992), pp. 3–7.

13 *Time* (November 11, 1991), p. 36. I am indebted to Carol Starcevic for showing me this article.

14 See Anthony Kimery, "Big Brother Wants to Look into Your Bank Account (Any Time it Pleases)," *Wired* 1: 6 (1993), pp. 91–3, 134.

15 Rob Kling, "Massively Parallel Computing and Information Capitalism," in Daniel Hillis and James Bailey, eds, *New Era of Computation* (Cambridge, MA: MIT Press, 1992), pp. 229–30.

16 David Lyon, in "Bentham's Panopticon: From Moral Architecture to Electronic Surveillance," *Queen's Quarterly* 98: 3 (1991), moderates the totalizing vision that is often drawn from this analysis: ". . . it is not so much that we are already enclosed in the cells of the electronic Panopticon, but that certain contemporary institutions display panoptic features. Panopticism is one tendency among other . . ." (p. 614).

17 "Claritas Corporation – An Overview," advertising material furnished by the company in 1991. I am grateful to Colin Fisher for showing me this text.

18 The clusters were listed in *USA Today* (March 16, 1989), p. 1B.

19 Colin Hay of Lancaster University suggested this line of inquiry to me. See his essay "Mobilisation Through Interpellation," *Social and Legal Studies* (forthcoming).

20 See Michel Foucault, "Governmentality," in *The Foucault Effect*, pp. 87–104.

21 Ibid., p. 92.

22 Jean-François Lyotard, *The Postmodern Condition*, trans. Geoff Bennington and Brian Massumi (Minneapolis: University of Minnesota Press, 1984), p. 67.

23 See Chantal Mouffe, "Democracy, Pluralism and Uncertainty"

(unpublished paper) and Ernesto Laclau, "Power and Representation," in Mark Poster, ed., *Politics, Theory and Contemporary Culture* (New York: Columbia University Press, 1993), pp. 277–96.

Notes to Chapter 6: Critical Theory and TechnoCulture: Habermas and Baudrillard

1 See Carol Johnson, "The Problem of Reformism and Marx's Theory of Fetishism," *New Left Review* No. 119 (1980), pp. 70–96, for a discussion of Marx's failure adequately to theorize the problem of revolutionary consciousness.
2 Karl Marx, "Theses on Feuerbach," in *Writings of the Young Marx on Philosophy and Society*, trans. and ed. L. Easton and K. Guddat (New York: Anchor, 1967), p. 400.
3 It could be argued that the Marxist school of historiography begun by E. P. Thompson with *The Making of the English Working Class* (London: Gollancz; New York: Random House, 1963) as well as the Birmingham School of cultural studies are exceptions, serious ones, to this charge.
4 See, for example, the long history of the effort to marry the ideas of Freud with those of Marx, e.g. Wilhelm Reich, "Dialectical Materialism and Psycho-analysis" (1929); Reuben Osborn, *Marxism and Psychoanalysis* (1965); Herbert Marcuse, *Eros and Civilization* (1955); etc.
5 Martin Jay begins to address this question in "Should Intellectual History Take a Linguistic Turn? Reflections on the Habermas–Gadamer Debate," in Dominick LaCapra and Steven Kaplan, eds, *Modern European Intellectual History* (Ithaca, NY: Cornell University Press, 1982), pp. 86–110.
6 Mark Poster, *The Mode of Information* (Cambridge: Polity Press; Chicago: University of Chicago Press, 1990).
7 The English version can be found in *Toward a Rational Society: Student Protest, Science, and Politics*, trans. Jeremy Shapiro (Boston: Beacon, 1971).
8 *Dialectic of Enlightenment*, trans. John Cumming (New York: Seabury, 1972).
9 *Toward a Rational Society*, p. 84.
10 Ibid., p. 91.
11 Jürgen Habermas, *The Theory of Communicative Action*, trans.

Thomas McCarthy, vols 1 and 2 (Cambridge: Polity Press; Boston: Beacon Press, 1984, 1987).

12 Jürgen Habermas, "Toward a Theory of Communicative Competence," in *Recent Sociology*, No. 2: *Patterns of Communicative Behavior*, ed. Hans Peter Dreitzel (New York: Macmillan, 1970), p. 144. This text is a translation of "Vorbereitende Bemerkungen zu einer Theorie der kommunikativen Kompetenz."

13 Ibid., p. 146.

14 *Communication and the Evolution of Society*, trans. Thomas McCarthy (Boston: Beacon Press, 1979), p. 148.

15 Habermas provides examples of this in *Communication*, p. 112.

16 On Habermas's disagreements with the left student movement in West Germany, see the first three chapters of *Toward a Rational Society*.

17 See Henri Lefebvre, *Everyday Life in the Modern World*, trans. Sacha Rabinovich (New York: Harper Torchbook, 1971), and *Le Langage et la société* (Paris: Gallimard, 1966). See also Roland Barthes, *Mythologies*, trans. Annette Lavers (New York: Hill & Wang, 1972), and *Système de la mode* (Paris: Seuil, 1967).

18 Semiology may be defined as the study of all social meanings, not just those inherent in language.

19 Jean Baudrillard, *La Société de consommation* (Paris: Gallimard, 1970), pp. 78–9. In Saussure's theory of structural linguistics signs are composed of signifiers or words and signifieds or mental images. Emphasis is placed on the relations between the signifiers, whose connection to signifieds and referents is virtually ignored.

20 For an example of that type of analysis, see Stuart Ewen, *Captains of Consciousness: Advertising and the Social Roots of the Consumer Culture* (New York: McGraw Hill, 1976).

21 *La Société de consommation*, p. 134.

22 Ibid., p. 188.

23 For numerous examples of analyses of ads, see Judith Williamson, *Decoding Advertisements* (London: Marion Boyars, 1978).

24 For more extensive elaborations of this sort of homological analysis, see Jean-Joseph Goux, *Economie et symbolique: Freud, Marx* (Paris: Seuil, 1973), and Marc Shell, *The Economy of Literature* (Baltimore: Johns Hopkins University Press, 1978).

25 *Pour une critique de l'économie politique du signe* (Paris: Gallimard, 1972) p. 181.

26 *The Mirror of Production*, trans. Mark Poster (St Louis: Telos Press, 1975), p. 17.

27 See the interview with Baudrillard by Maria Shevtsova, "Intellectuals [sic] Commitment and Political Power," in *Thesis Eleven* Nos 10–11 (1984–5), pp. 166–75. Baudrillard presents his current views on politics. Also interesting in this regard is Robert Maniquis, "Une conversation avec Jean Baudrillard," *UCLA French Studies* vols 2–3 (1984–5), pp. 1–22.

28 It might be noted that Baudrillard defends the notion of the symbolic against psychological theories. See his critique of psychoanalysis in "Beyond the Unconscious: the Symbolic," *Discourse* vol. 3 (1981), pp. 60–87.

29 See Jürgen Habermas, *The Theory of Communicative Action*, vol. 1: *Reason and the Rationalization of Society*, trans. Thomas McCarthy (Cambridge: Polity Press; Boston: Beacon, 1984); originally published in 1981.

30 See Baudrillard, "Fatality or Reversible Imminence: Beyond the Uncertainty Principle," *Social Research* 49: 2 (1982), pp. 272–93, for a discussion of the chance/necessity distinction in relation to the world of hyper-reality.

31 See Hal Foster, ed., *The Anti-Aesthetic: Essays on Postmodern Culture* (Port Townsend, WA: Bay Press, 1983), especially the brilliant piece by Fredric Jameson. It might be noted that Baudrillard himself is a contributor to this collection.

32 See also Jean Baudrillard, *A l'ombre des majorités silencieuses . . .* (Paris: Utopie, 1978); available in English as *In the Shadow of the Silent Majority* (New York: Semiotext(e), 1983).

33 See Baudrillard's essays "What Are You Doing After the Orgy?," *Artforum* (October 1983), pp. 42–6; "Astral America," *Artforum* (September 1984), pp. 70–4; and *L'Amérique* (Paris: Grasset, 1985) for descriptions of life in the new world of the media, especially in the United States where the tendencies Baudrillard discusses are most advanced.

34 Michel de Certeau, *The Practice of Everyday Life*, trans. Steven Rendell (Berkeley: University of California Press, 1984). See also Pierre Bourdieu, *La Distinction: critique sociale du jugement* (Paris: Minuit, 1979), trans. Richard Nice (Cambridge, MA: Harvard University Press, 1984).

35 See Jean Baudrillard, *L'Echange symbolique et la mort* (Paris:

Gallimard, 1976) and *A l'ombre des majorités silencieuses . . .*
(Paris: Utopie, 1978).
36 *Toward a Rational Society*, p. 37.
37 Ibid., p. 61.
38 *Pour une critique de l'économie politique du signe*, p. 218.

Notes to Chapter 7: Politics in the Mode of Information: Spike Lee's *Do the Right Thing*

This chapter benefited from the comments, criticisms and suggestions
of many individuals, most notably Lyndon Barrett, Lilian Manzor-
Coats, Jon Wiener and Linda Williams. It was presented as a paper at
a University of California Irvine History Department colloquium, a
Seminar on the Diversity of Language at the University of Pennsylva-
nia, a Conference on Intercultural Communication at UC San Diego,
the Minority Discourse conference at the UC Humanities Research
Institute, and at the Institute for Study in the Arts at Arizona State
University. I am grateful to the participants at these events who
offered their advice.

1 Almost one year later, on April 28, 1993, Lee finally did appear.
   Linking his film to the civil disturbance of a year earlier, Lee said
   ". . . I understood when I wrote *Do the Right Thing* that people
   would react the way they did in that film when they saw an
   unarmed black man killed by police" (*Los Angeles Times*, April
   29, 1993, p. F2).
2 *The Practice of Everyday Life*, trans. Steven Rendell (Berkeley:
   University of California Press, 1984).
3 *New York Times*, January 19, 1885, p. 4. I came across the
   article first in William Pietz, "The Phonograph in Africa," in
   Geoff Bennington et al., eds, *Poststructuralism and the Question
   of History* (New York: Cambridge University Press, 1987), pp.
   268–9.
4 See, for example, Dick Hebdige, *Cut 'n' Mix: Culture, Identity
   and Caribbean Music* (New York: Methuen, 1987), p. 26, and
   Les Back, "Coughing up Fire," *New Formations* 5 (1988), pp.
   141–52. For the role of music in black anti-racist politics in
   England, see Paul Gilroy, *There Ain't No Black in the Union
   Jack* (London: Hutchinson, 1987), pp. 120–35 and *passim*. For
   interesting discussions of the history of black music, with no

particular focus on technology, see Paul Oliver, ed., *Black Music in Britain* (Milton Keynes and Philadelphia: Open University Press, 1990). I am indebted to James Clifford and Lisa Lowe for telling me about these works.

5   *Cut 'n' Mix*, p. 37.
6   Ibid., p. 83.
7   On the international character of black music, its weaving of different traditions that cut across national boundaries, see Paul Gilroy, "Cultural Studies and Ethnic Absolutism," in Lawrence Grossberg et al., eds, *Cultural Studies* (New York: Routledge, 1992), pp. 187–8.
8   *Cut 'n' Mix*, pp. 128–9.
9   Les Back, "Coughing up Fire," p. 142.
10 Theodor Adorno, "On the Fetish Character in Music and the Regression of Listening," in Andrew Arato et al., eds, *The Essential Frankfurt School Reader* (New York: Urizen, 1978), pp. 270–99.
11 Paul Gilroy, *There Ain't No Black in the Union Jack*, p. 165.
12 Ibid., p. 150.
13 *Cut 'n' Mix*, pp. 154–5.
14 Isaac Julien's *Young Soul Rebels* is of interest in this regard.
15 Richard Corliss, "Boyz of New Black City," *Time* (June 17, 1991), pp. 64–8, and John Powers, "Mixed Doubles," *LA Weekly* (June 7–13, 1991), pp. 33–5, both underscore the role of *Do the Right Thing* in the revival of black cinema, as do Zeinabu Irene Davis in "Black Independent or Hollywood Iconoclast?," *Cineaste* 17: 4, pp. 36–7, and Robert Sklar in "What is the Right Thing?," *Cineaste* 17: 4, pp. 32–3.
16 Wahneema Lubiano, "But Compared to What?," *Black American Literature Forum* 25: 2 (1991), pp. 253–82.
17 This has been noted by many reviewers. See, for example, Ellen Goodman, "Women in Spike Lee's World," *The Washington Post* (July 18, 1989), p. A23, and Michele Wallace, "Invisibility Blues," *Artforum* 28: 2 (1989), pp. 19–22.
18 J. Hoberman argues otherwise that *Do the Right Thing* presents no essential divisions within the black community. See "Pass/Fail," *The Village Voice* (July 11, 1989), p. 62.
19 Thomas Doherty, review of *Do the Right Thing*, *Film Quarterly* 43: 2 (1989–90), p. 38.
20 Spike Lee, *Do the Right Thing* (New York: Fireside, 1989), pp. 190–1.

21   Ibid., pp. 243–4.
22   Homi Bhabha, "The Other Question," in Francis Barker et al.,
     eds, *Literature, Politics and Theory* (New York: Methuen,
     1986), pp. 161ff. Also see, by Homi Bhabha, "Signs Taken as
     Wonders," in Henry Gates, ed., *"Race," Writing, and Difference*
     (Chicago: University of Chicago Press, 1985), pp. 163–84; "Of
     Mimicry and Man: The Ambivalence of Colonial Discourse,"
     October 28 (Spring 1984), pp. 125–33; and "The Commitment
     to Theory," *New Formations* 5 (Summer 1988), pp. 5–24.
23   For an analysis of Marx's use of the term "fetishism," see Will-
     iam Pietz, "Fetishism and Dialectical Materialism," in Emily
     Apter and William Pietz, eds, *Fetishism as a Cultural Discourse:
     Gender, Commodity, Vision* (Ithaca, NY: Cornell University
     Press, 1991).
24   Arjun Appadurai, "Disjuncture and Difference in the Global
     Cultural Economy," in *Public Culture* 2: 2 (1990), pp. 1–24.
25   bell hooks, "Counterhegemonic Art: The Right Thing," *Z*
     (October 1989), p. 32. For another African-American perspec-
     tive, this one a critique of the film as fascist and racist, see
     Stanley Crouch, "Do the Race Thing," *The Village Voice* (June
     20, 1989), pp. 73–4, 76.
26   For an argument of the general impact of technologically medi-
     ated music in this direction, see John Mowitt, "The Sound of
     Music in the Era of its Electronic Reproducibility," in Richard
     Lepperd and Susan McClary, eds, *Music and Society* (New
     York: Cambridge University Press, 1987), pp. 173–97.
27   Emily Apter, *Feminizing the Fetish: Psychoanalysis and Narra-
     tive Obsession in Turn-of-the-Century France* (Ithaca, NY:
     Cornell University Press, 1991).
28   Paul Gilroy, *There Ain't No Black*, p. 217.
29   Tejumola Olaniyan, " 'Uplift the Race!': *Coming to America, Do
     the Right Thing*, and the Poetics and Politics of 'Othering',"
     unpublished manuscript, p. 26.
30   Ernesto Laclau, "Power and Representation," in Mark Poster,
     ed., *Politics, Theory and Contemporary Culture* (New York:
     Columbia University Press, 1993), p. 291.

Notes to Chapter 8:   RoboBody

1   Eric Rentschler was most helpful in suggesting to me relevant
     studies on film and cultural criticism in general.

2 Bill Nichols, "The Work of Culture in the Age of Cybernetic Systems," *Screen* (Winter 1988), pp. 22–47, is very insightful about these processes.

3 There are many ways to formulate these changes. For one different from my own, see Friedrich Kittler, "Gramophone, Film, Typewriter," *October* 41 (Summer 1987), pp. 101–18.

4 Other works of a similar type are *Terminator, Blade Runner, Scanners* and the short-lived TV series *Max Headroom*.

5 Among the interesting studies of the android figure, see: Donna Haraway, "A Manifesto for Cyborgs: Science, Technology, and Socialist Feminism in the 1980s," *Socialist Review* 80 (March–April 1985), pp. 65–107; Gabriele Schwab, "Cyborgs: Postmodern Phantasms of Body and Mind," *Discourse* 9 (Spring–Summer 1987), pp. 64–84; Patricia Mellencamp, "Oedipus and the Robot in *Metropolis*," *Enclitic* 5: 1 (1981), pp. 20–42; Janet Bergstrom, "Androids and Androgyny," *camera obscura* 15 (1986), pp. 37–64; Andreas Huyssen, "The Vamp and the Machine: Technology and Sexuality in Fritz Lang's *Metropolis*," *New German Critique* 24–5 (Fall–Winter 1981–2), pp. 221–37.

6 Jean Baudrillard, "The Ecstasy of Communication," in Hal Foster, ed., *The Anti-Esthetic* (Port Townsend, WA: Bay Press, 1983), pp. 128–9.

Notes to Chapter 9: What Does Wotan Want? Ambivalent Feminism in Wagner's *Ring*

1 On the relation of Wagner's work to the medieval epics, see R. G. Finch, "The Icelandic and German Sources of Wagner's *Ring of the Nibelung*," *Leeds Studies in English* 17 (1986), pp. 1–23.

2 For an interesting study of that production, see J. J. Nattiez, *Tétralogies: Wagner, Boulez, Chereau: essai sur l'infidélité* (Paris: Christian Bourgeois, 1983). On the relation of Wagner's family to productions of the *Ring* at Bayreuth, see Samuel Lipman, "Wagner's Holy Family," *Commentary* (November 1978), pp. 68–73.

3 The classic work of Wagner criticism which combines both strategies is Theodor Adorno, *In Search of Wagner*, trans.

Rodney Livingstone (London: New Left Books, 1981). Adorno revised some of his harsher judgments of this essay, especially concerning Wagner's music, in "L'actualité de Wagner," *La Musique en jeu* 22 (1976), pp. 80–93.

4 Samuel Weber, "Opera and Dramaturgy in Frankfurt: Dossier (II) Taking Place: Towards a Theater of Dislocation," *Enclitic* 8: 1–2 (1984), p. 133. For another effective literary analysis of a Wagnerian music drama, see Northrop Frye, "The World as Music and Idea in Wagner's *Parsifal*," *Carleton Germanic Papers* 12 (1984), pp. 37–49. Wagner also had some influence on literary figures. For the case of James Joyce, see Timothy P. Martin, "Joyce, Wagner and the Artist-Hero," *Journal of Modern Literature* 11: 1 (1984), pp. 66–88. For the case of Thomas Mann, see Gail Finney, "Self-Reflexive Siblings: Incest as Narcissism in Tieck, Wagner, and Thomas Mann," *German Quarterly* 56: 2 (1983), pp. 243–54. There is also an issue of Wagner's theory of language in relation to music. On this, see Helene M. Kastinger Riley, "Some German Theories on the Origin of Language from Herder to Wagner," *Modern Language Review* 74 (1979), pp. 617–23. On Wagner's preference for integrating literature and music over program music, see Carl Dahlhaus, "Wagner and Program Music," *Studies in Romanticism* 9 (1970), pp. 3–20.

5 Philippe Lacoue-Labarthe, "Baudelaire *contra* Wagner," *Etudes Françaises* 17: 3–4 (1981), pp. 23–52.

6 Samuel Weber, in "Opera and Dramaturgy," argues on the contrary, "Precisely this Enlightenment ideal of the autonomous subject is what the *Ring* plays out in all of its self-destructive circularity . . ." (p. 139).

7 George Bernard Shaw, *The Perfect Wagnerite: A Commentary on the Niblung's Ring* (New York: Dover, 1967), first publication 1898.

8 Sigmund Freud, *New Introductory Lectures*, trans. James Strachey (New York: Norton, 1965), p. 112.

9 In a letter to Röckel, Wagner characterizes Wotan as "the pinnacle of intelligence at the present time" (cited in Jean Nurdin, "La résurrection de l'Europe par le Wagnérisme," *Les Langues Modernes* 73 [1979], pp. 494–501). If Wagner is right that Wotan represents the European intellectual, my argument does not work very well.

10 Jacques Derrida, *Spurs: Nietzsche's Styles*, trans. Barbara

Harlow (Chicago: University of Chicago Press, 1979). René Girard, "Superman in the Underground: Strategies of Madness – Nietzsche, Wagner and Dostoevsky," *Modern Language Notes* 91 (1976), pp. 1257–66, interprets Nietzsche's writing differently, based in part on the complex psychodynamics of his relation with Wagner.

11   *The Case of Wagner*, trans. Walter Kaufman (New York: Vintage, 1967), p. 160.

12   Ibid., p. 183.

13   Ibid., p. 185.

14   Ibid., p. 166, where Nietzsche writes: "Wagner's *success* – his success with nerves and consequently women . . . "

15   Ibid., p. 163.

16   Richard Wagner, *The Ring of the Nibelung*, trans. Andrew Porter (New York: Norton, 1976), p. 19.

17   *The Ring*, p. 32.

18   *The Ring*, p. 70. Philip Friedheim, "Wagner and the Aesthetics of the Scream," *19th Century Music* 7 (1983), pp. 63–70, raises an interesting issue of the relation of the will to "the scream." He does not, however, carry out this analysis in relation to Wotan's discussions of his will.

19   *The Ring*, p. 109.

20   *The Ring*, p. 109.

21   *The Ring*, p. 140.

22   *The Ring*, p. 146.

23   *The Ring*, pp. 224–5.

24   *The Ring*, p. 225.

25   See George Bernard Shaw, *The Perfect Wagnerite: A Commentary on the Niblung's Ring* (New York: Dover, 1967). For an evaluation of Shaw's interpretation, see Thomas D. O'Sullivan, "*The Perfect Wagnerite*: Shaw's Reading of the *Ring*," *English Literature in Transition* 30: 1 (1987), pp. 39–47.

26   This is reported in Thomas Mann, *Pro and Contra Wagner*, trans. Allan Blunden (Chicago: University of Chicago Press, 1985), p. 221 (original edition, *Wagner und unsere Zeit* [Frankfurt: Fischer, 1963]). David C. Large, in "The Political Background of the Foundation of the Bayreuth Festival, 1876," *Central European History* 11 (1978), pp. 162–72, shows a contrary conservative influence of politics through the financial sponsorship of music in Bismarckian Germany.

27   Mann, *Pro and Contra Wagner*, pp. 171–93.

28 Ludwig Feuerbach, *The Essence of Christianity*, trans. George Eliot (New York: Harper & Row, 1957).

29 George C. Windell, "Hegel, Feuerbach, and Wagner's *Ring*," *Central European History* 9 (1976), pp. 27–57, takes this approach.

30 For a detailed study of the composition of the *Ring*, see Robert Bailey, "The Structure of the *Ring* and its Evolution," *19th Century Music* 1 (1977), pp. 48–61, and "Wagner's Sketches for Siegfrieds Tod," in Harold Powers, ed., *Studies in Music History: Essays for Oliver Strunk* (Princeton, NJ: Princeton University Press, 1968). For a more general understanding of Wagner's position in his cultural epoch from the historian's vantage point, see David Large and William Weber, eds, *Wagnerism in European Culture and Politics* (Ithaca, NY: Cornell University Press, 1984). See also Kenneth G. Chapman, "Siegfried and Brünnhilde and the Passage of Time in Wagner's Ring," *Current Musicology* 32 (1981), pp. 43–58, on the relation of the length of composition to the unity of time in the work.

31 For the best statement of this perspective, see George Windell, "Hegel, Feuerbach, and Wagner's *Ring*," *Central European History* 11 (1977), pp. 27–57. Windell insists on the influence of Hegel on the *Ring* even more than that of Feuerbach. Another intellectual historian, Carl Schorske, tries to clarify the issue of influence by comparing Wagner with William Morris. See "The Quest for the Grail: Wagner and Morris," in K. Wolff and Barrington Moore, Jr., eds, *The Critical Spirit: Essays in Honor of Herbert Marcuse* (Boston: Beacon Press, 1967), pp. 216–32. Hugh Ridley, "Myth as Illusion or Cognition: Feuerbach, Wagner and Nietzsche," *German Life and Letters* 34 (1980), pp. 74–80, argues for the salience of a Feuerbachian concept of "myth" in the *Ring*.

32 The ablest proponent is L. J. Rather, *The Dream of Self-Destruction: Wagner's Ring and the Modern World* (Baton Rouge: Louisiana State University Press, 1979).

33 Ibid., p. 63.

34 Ibid., pp. 84–5.

35 Ibid., p. 105.

36 Ibid., p. 135.

37 Ibid., p. 174. Another criticism of this position is found in Friedrich Kittler, "World-Breath: On Wagner's Media Technology," in *Opera Through Other Eyes*, pp. 215–35, which at-

tributes political significance to Wagner's innovations in the staging of the operas.

38 Louis Althusser, *For Marx*, trans. Ben Brewster (New York: Vintage, 1970).

39 Theodor Adorno, *Philosophy of Modern Music*, trans. Anne Mitchell and Wesley Blomster (New York: Seabury, 1980), p. 24.

40 Friedrich Nietzsche, *The Birth of Tragedy and the Case of Wagner*, trans. Walter Kaufman (New York: Vintage, 1967), pp. 153–92. For an opposing view, see Ray Furness, "Wagner and Decadence," *German Life and Letters* 35: 3 (1982), pp. 229–37.

41 *The Ring*, p. 19.

42 Ibid., p. 106.

43 Ibid.

44 Ibid., p. 224.

45 For critical views of Wagner's effort at a total art work, see Theodor Adorno, *In Search of Wagner*, trans. Rodney Livingstone (London: New Left Books, 1981), and Andreas Huyssen's treatment of Adorno's Wagner in "Adorno in Reverse: From Hollywood to Richard Wagner," *New German Critique* 29 (Spring–Summer 1983), pp. 8–38. Far less interesting is Jacques Barzun, *Darwin, Marx, Wagner: Critique of a Heritage* (Chicago: University of Chicago Press, 1981).

46 Adorno, *In Search of Wagner*, p. 15.

47 Ibid., p. 101.

48 Ibid., p. 100.

49 Ibid., p. 113.

Index